GOD'S SEARCH FOR US
Five Truths from a Missing Coin

Fr. Jeffrey Kirby, STD

PONTIFEX UNIVERSITY PRESS

Pontifex University Press
310 San Carlos Ave.
El Cerrito, CA.
94530

ISBN: 978 1 729 21760 3

Cover design: Charlie Deist
Cover image: Domenico Fetti, *Parable of the Lost Drachma* (c. 1618)

To the Parishioners of Our Lady of Grace

Indian Land, South Carolina

CONTENTS

INTRODUCTION

A Lost Inheritance

Western culture has eclipsed the fundamental conviction that developed its worldview, gave birth to its institutions, and provided continual rejuvenation to its way of life, namely, that the living God – All-Powerful and All-Knowing – is actively searching for us. In this radical quest, God became a man, lived a human life, died a torturous death, triumphantly rose from the dead, and ascended into eternal glory. This central Christian belief is the heart of Western culture. It broke the pathetic, pantheistic, and deterministic pagan worldview of angry, vengeful gods in a dark world of personal despair and meaninglessness. It was precisely the Dawn from on High breaking upon the human family and shedding abundant, eternal light that allowed for a hope to be born, a dignity recognized, and a human creativity to flourish. It made all the difference. And it gave an impetus to the creation and development of Western culture.

As this profound belief has waned, so have its blessings. As we see a formerly abandoned worldview – with all its demons – being ushered back into Western culture, we have to make some decisions. Will the diminishing of the light be recognized? Will darkness be rejected? There are many options to preserve the West. And yet, if Western people pursue all other options, but forget the most foundational, then the result would only be a house built on sand. The Sacred Scriptures remind us:

If the Lord does not build the house,
>   it is useless for the builders to work on it.

If the Lord does not protect a city,
>   it is useless for the guard to stay alert.

(Psalm 127:1)

Christian believers and institutions, therefore, are especially called to bring the reality of the Incarnation and Paschal Mystery to the forefront of public awareness and sensitivity. For this to happen, believers and Christian bodies need to deepen their own understanding, appreciation, integration, and comfortability with these truths of faith. Society attempts to silence, shame, privatize and trivialize Christian beliefs, practices and influence. The best way to approach and deflect this attempt is through personal lives, marriages and families, and faith-based organizations that are intentionally and holistically living in the light of the Incarnation and Paschal Mystery.

In an effort to give this response, it is pressing that believers and Christian culture dive into the richness of the Sacred Scriptures, indulge in the life-giving spiritual patrimony of the Church, and invest themselves in holy fellowship with one another, and selfless service to the poor and sick. This observation leads us to a parable. Imitating the Lord's own pedagogy, we turn to a story. From this story, we will draw five truths that can help each of us to renew and deepen our own acceptance and assimilation of the declarations: "And the Word became flesh and dwelt among us," (John 1:14) and "Christ has died, Christ is Risen, Christ will come again" (cf. 1 Cor 15:26).

In the public ministry of Jesus Christ, the Lord taught the crowds and served the sick. On one such occasion, he described a common household experience. The Lord taught:

Or suppose a woman has ten silver coins and loses one. Doesn't she light a lamp, sweep the house and search carefully until she finds it? And when she finds it, she calls her friends and neighbors together and says, 'Rejoice with me; I have found my lost coin' (Luke 15:8-9).

While the example is a mundane and ordinary one, it is a personal and effective one. It touches upon the intimacy of family life and the ins and outs of daily living. From this story, so enduring and relatable, five lessons can be drawn. In order to appreciate these five lessons, the movement within the story needs to be punctuated. The movement includes: a) A lost coin and the woman who searches for it; b) The woman lights a lamp for her search; c) The woman sweeps the house looking for the coin; d) The woman finds the coin and calls together her friends; and, e) The woman invites her friends to celebrate and rejoice with her.

The Lord recounts a movement within the scene in order to describe how God has searched for humanity through the generations. The story emphasizes the principal truth of the Judeo-Christian tradition; namely, God is searching for humanity.[1] While contemporary philosophy may rightly explore humanity's search for God (or the transcendental truths through which he might be known),[2] the radical claim of the Jewish faith – from which the Lord Jesus came – is the same claim incarnated by his presence among us, specifically, that God is looking for humanity. This is a powerful truth that reveals the very heart of the human person's identity. It is best summarized by Pope Benedict XVI who taught:

We are not some casual and meaningless product of evolution. Each of us is the result of a thought of God. Each of us is willed, each of us is loved, each of us is necessary.[3]

As the woman in the story desperately and carefully searches for the lost coin, lighting a lamp and sweeping the house, so God is passionately and attentively searching for humanity, a humanity that is easily lost in itself by false or incomplete knowledge, confusion, error, and sin. When a person allows himself to be found by God, he calls that person to a greater fellowship with himself and with others. This deep fellowship leads the person into a new life of love and peace, to a great celebration and rejoicing in God.

Five Essential Truths

The five truths that can be discerned in this story explore the ways in which God seeks out all people. In turn, the Church receives a mandate within this work of God. As such, the Church seeks to present Christian beliefs and moral truth, even within the pluralistic environments of the West, which were inspired and established by these very truths. In this effort, the Church is greatly assisted by philosophical truths that can be drawn from her theological teachings.

The five truths that were chosen were selected precisely because they are the most observable and debated in contemporary culture, and in many ways, they are the ones that current cultural trends attempt to redefine the most. These five truths are deeply inspired by the woman of the Gospel, since the parable clearly displays God's initiative and action toward the human family. These truths are presented here in the same movement given by the Gospel narrative.

First Truth: As the woman searches for the missing coin, so God carefully searches for us. God's search for us reveals to us the dynamics of the interior life of the Holy Trinity. God does not dwell as three isolated persons in need of external fellowship, but as three distinct interrelated persons who live for one another as a true communion of persons, as a divine family, infinitely perfect and

4

blessed in himself. This truth about the interior life of the Holy Trinity teaches us a proper sense of integrated, personal autonomy.

Second Truth: The woman in the story lit a lamp as she looked for the coin. In a plan of sheer goodness, God lit a lamp and created us to share in his goodness and love. As we turned away from him and chose a wayward path, God the Son, the Second Person of the Trinity, came and actively searched for us. He came as the Light of the world. And the distinctiveness of his personhood, rather than a cause of self-sovereignty, was a move toward service and was an act of self-donation to God the Father and to humanity. This truth reveals how the God the Son, who lived a fully human life, shows humanity what it means to be human, what the meaning of suffering is, and what is the true meaning of service and care for others.

Third Truth: The woman vigorously swept her house as she looked for the missing coin. So, in his ministry among us, the Lord swept the household of faith. As he fulfilled the promises and prophecies given to Israel, he taught humanity what to look for in the Savior and what it meant to follow him. As the Lord exercised his public ministry, crowds assembled around him and were intrigued by his words and deeds. As he swept away false understandings of his day, which would eventually lead to moral theories relating to materialism, individualism, and utilitarianism, the Lord taught and displayed what it means to live a fully human life and what it means to be one of his disciples. He gave an example of a virtuous life, especially in service to others, such as the sick and those in need.

By his life and teachings, the Lord gave a compelling invitation to the crowds to live beyond the isolation and meaninglessness created by self- absorption and wayward egos, and to live fully as human persons beyond themselves: to deny their own comfort, take up their crosses, and follow him (Luke 18:18-30). Few chose to pursue and accompany

5

him on such an adventure. This truth illustrates the Lord's perfect witness and argues for the importance of virtue and goodness in human life.

Fourth Truth: Upon finding the coin, the woman called together her friends. As some people within the crowds accepted the call to discipleship, the Lord summoned them together into a community and appointed twelve apostles with a mission to teach and serve others as he was doing. The apostles, and their successors the bishops, are to shepherd the community of disciples as they hold the Lord's own teaching office. No one person, nor his opinions, has a monopoly over the truth. No disciple has the power to determine truth on his own but is called to discern truth within the community of faith, to accept and wrestle with the teachings that are collegially given by the magisterium of the Church in Christ's name.

As the Lord taught in both words and deeds, likewise is the magisterium to teach throughout the generations until the Lord returns. Thus, the magisterium is a teacher, both to the community of faith and to the world as it exemplifies the traits, posture, and confidence of the Good Teacher. This truth emphasizes the need for a teacher in desiring moral goodness and seeking peace of heart.

Fifth Truth: After the woman called together her friends, she invited them to celebrate and rejoice with her. In a similar fashion, as the Lord calls together his followers into a community and appoints a teaching authority, he invites the community to celebrate, rejoicing in the new life and freedom that has been given to them. The summit and source of this celebration is the Eucharistic offering (Luke 24:13-35). The glory of God is the human person fully alive, and alive within a community that both loves and is loved by him. No fully abundant life can be found within any one person by himself. The Christian faith manifests this basic human truth that people are called together by nature and faith to be in a community, and to be approached with love and respect. As Pope St. John Paul II taught: "A person is an entity of a sort to which the only proper and adequate way to relate is love."[4] This truth manifests the importance of community life in discerning and living by faith and virtue.

A Needed Clarity

These basic theological and human truths need emphasis today, especially as the Church seeks to fulfill her call to reveal the Face of God and to guide humanity in his ways. It is the hope of the Church that humanity will openly listen and engage in dialogue with her, as she fulfills her mission in our world today. These truths are especially timely since the Western world appears to be confused about the identity and dignity of the human person and the importance of community life. There is a deficiency when it comes to a developed understanding of personal identity, selfless service, freedom and virtue, and the basic need of people to be in a community, namely, to be loved and to love within an intimate bond of people and relationships. These have been lost, or are being lost, because the loving pursuit by God toward each person has been ignored, taken for granted, dismissed as insignificant, or completely denied.

To the Reader

And so, dear reader, why this book? How can it help you? How can it assist you to help others?

This simple book is a reminder of forgotten realities, a resource to reinvigorate a tired culture, and a re-assertion of the radical truth that God is searching for us. Yes, this book is a small effort to point to a supreme truth: namely, that the living God – the Creator and Sustainer of all things – will move any mountain or fill any valley to find us, heal and restore us, embrace us, and show us our dignity as his children.

The chapters of this book, therefore, were written to provide you with foundational truths that can serve as a light to your own life, as well as leaven to Western culture. These truths will compel you to look at the Church as both Mother and Teacher, Community and Mystical Body. The acceptance and living out of these truths will strengthen you to be witnesses of God's love for humanity and equip you to be carriers of this transformative message to the ends of the earth.

And so, with this mission in mind, we now make a mini-pilgrimage through the five chapters of the book. Each chapter explains and develops one of our basic truths and then shows us the priority and importance of this truth in human life and civilized culture. Our journey begins. Enjoy the adventure. Accept the truth. Live the mission.

CHAPTER ONE

AUTONOMY AND THE INTERIOR LIFE OF THE HOLY TRINITY

Introduction

The Church humbly approaches the mystery of the Holy Trinity and patiently discerns various lessons about personhood from God himself. These lessons can teach and form anyone of good will, the identity of the human person, as well as the richness of human life and the purpose and place of authentic autonomy. These lessons on personhood rightly show the human family the proper role that autonomy plays within a call to self-donation and community life.

The Apophatic Tradition and Revelation

In seeing the woman who searches for the missing coin, we see a reflection of the presence and work of the Holy Trinity within human history. This divine work, through the course of the ages, is an overflowing of the love that eternally exists within the inner life of the Trinity.[5] As Pope Benedict XVI reminded the Church:

> God is Love... everything has its origin in God's love, everything is shaped by it, everything is directed towards it. Love is God's greatest gift to humanity, it is his promise and our hope.[6]

In the midst of such a divine identity and action, how are we to understand God? How can we seek to comprehend him and his work among us?

Certainly, God is Mystery. He is not merely a mystery as the empirical sciences understand it, meaning something that we have not yet "figured out." God is a mystery that cannot be fully understood by created beings within their own power. If we claim to understand God fully, then we would ourselves be God, having our own peculiar divine identity.[7] The apophatic tradition of the Church therefore describes the mystery of God in many ways, such as "deep calls out to deep" and the "cloud of unknowing." Whatever is said about God, he is infinitely more.[8] How then are we to know God? Is he knowable? By what power can creation claim to know him at all?

Revelation Known by Reason

From the depth of his Mystery, God chose to make himself known in an act of freedom and love. He unveils himself to the world. As the Second Vatican Council taught: "In His goodness and wisdom God chose to reveal Himself and to make known to us the hidden purpose of His will."[9] This revelation began in creation itself when he manifested his love by making the world. He crowned his creation with the human person made "in his own image" endowed with a body and rational soul, consisting of an intellect and will.[10] As Pope John Paul II taught in his first encyclical:

> The Church cannot abandon man... We are speaking precisely of each man on this planet, this earth that the Creator gave to the first man, saying to the man and the woman: "subdue it and have dominion." Each man in all the unrepeatable reality of what he is and what he does, of his intellect and will, of his conscience and heart. Man who in his

reality has, because he is a "person," a history of his life that is his own and, most important, a history of his soul that is his own.[11]

This first grace of a rational soul allows humanity to know God through the natural light of reason.[12] The image of "light" is dominant in the tradition since God's mystery is usually depicted as a darkness of unknowing.[13] The use of the natural light of reason, therefore, is able to lead the human person to a natural revelation of who God is and to a natural theology that seeks to understand him.[14] What truths of God can natural reason disclose? Are these truths important? What role, if any, can they play in humanity's pursuit of happiness?

Natural reason allows the human person and community to know of the existence of an Absolute Being (whom we call God) and that we are contingent beings (namely, that we are creatures).[15] Reason can also indicate the goodness of God and the beauty of creation. More specifically, in terms of God, natural reason could allow the human mind to know that God is one, that he is all-powerful and all-knowing. The natural light of reason can also show the person the natural order of creation, the foundation of human dignity, and the role and importance of the human body. In grasping these natural truths, the person in community and the community together can begin to discern moral goodness and recognize the imperatives born from such goodness as a means to fulfillment and happiness.

The reflection that leads to an acknowledgment of these truths is essential to human maturity as well as to a genuine notion of equality among human persons. These natural truths serve as a great equalizer since they apply to all: God is the God of all people and the commands born from natural goodness are obligatory for everyone.[16] Can these natural truths be fully trusted? Is natural theology a

11

consistent and trustworthy source for truth about God and moral goodness?

Certainly, natural theology – as the exercise of human reason – is only an attempt by the person to understand God, the person himself, and the world around him. Compared to supernatural revelation, it is similar to a person groping in the dark with nothing but a flickering light. The light flickers because of the fallen state of humanity and of reason. Left to its own device, reason will betray its goodness and choose a less noble good, or even something evil. Human reason is very impressionable and can be easily deceived or moved by negative influences within the cultural and societal views of its age. Reason is a powerful faculty of the human person, but one with limitations and weaknesses. As Pope Pius XII taught in his encyclical *Humani Generis*:

> Now the human intellect, in gaining the knowledge of such truths is hampered both by the activity of the senses and the imagination, and by evil passions arising from original sin. Hence men easily persuade themselves in such matters that what they do not wish to believe is false or at least doubtful.[17]

With this influence, is natural theology enough of a help for humanity to know God, personhood, and the world? If not, where can humanity turn for clear answers? How can the human family come to know the God who searches for it? How can humanity know who God truly is? In what way can the human family know for certain what is right and what is wrong?

Supernatural Revelation

Since knowledge of God, or of any person, cannot remain on the basic level of observation or analysis by reason, God chose to give humanity a supernatural revelation, which is revelation "above reason." This is a disclosure by God which human reason could not arrive at by its own power. It is God freely unveiling himself and sharing his own knowledge of himself with humanity. As the Second Vatican Council proclaimed:

> Through divine revelation, God chose to show forth and communicate Himself and the eternal decisions of His will regarding the salvation of men. That is to say, He chose to share with them those divine treasures which totally transcend the understanding of the human mind.[18]

It is precisely these truths, given by supernatural revelation, that allow humanity to have an intimate knowledge and relationship with God. As the philosopher Blaise Pascal recorded during his mystical Night of Fire: He is 'God of Abraham, God of Isaac, God of Jacob,' not of philosophers and scholars.[19] What truths, then, has God given by supernatural revelation? What knowledge has he given of himself that can help humanity to understand Him, personhood, and moral goodness?

God as Personal Being

The first truth that is supernaturally revealed to humanity is that God is a personal deity,[20] not a removed watch-maker, a random cosmic force, or an obsessive judge. God truly desires fellowship with all human persons. He is personal, and he loves and cares for humanity.[21] God's love, however, must be seen within the perspective of his divine identity. It is not an indication of weakness or need. God's love is not a sign of a flaw within himself. A fallen and incomplete notion of love was believed and taught by the ancient Greeks. The story of Love's birth as a weakness is told by Diotima in Plato's *Symposium:*

> On the birthday of Aphrodite there was a feast of the gods, at

13

which the god Plenty, who is the son of Discretion, was one of the guests. When the feast was over, Poverty, as the manner is on such occasions, came about the doors to beg. Now Plenty, who was the worse for nectar (there was no wine in those days), went into the garden of Zeus and fell into a heavy sleep; and Poverty considering her own straitened circumstances, plotted to have a child by him, and accordingly she lay down at his side and conceived Love, who partly because he is naturally a lover of the beautiful, and because Aphrodite is herself beautiful, and also because he was born on her birthday, is her follower and attendant.

The account continues:

And as his parentage is, so also are his fortunes. In the first place he is always poor, and anything but tender and fair, as the many imagine him; and he is rough and squalid, and has no shoes, nor a house to dwell in; on the bare earth exposed he lies under the open heaven, in the streets, or at the doors of houses, taking his rest; and like his mother he is always in distress. Like his father too, whom he also partly resembles, he is always plotting against the fair and good; he is bold, enterprising, strong, a mighty hunter, always weaving some intrigue or other, keen in the pursuit of wisdom, fertile in resources; a philosopher at all times, terrible as an enchanter, sorcerer, sophist.[22]

Contrary to such incomplete views of love, the revelation of God's love is a revelation of God himself. In knowing the revealed God, love is not a privation, but rather an abundance. God created humanity in order to share the richness of what he already possessed within himself. But how is this possible? How can God contain the fullness of love without being in a relationship with another? Is God an isolated Being? If so, how can we know about love and relationship from God?

God can indeed teach humanity about relationship and show it the full depth of love, because God is not an isolated Being – he exists as three distinct persons with one substance of divinity. In addition to the revelation that God is a personal deity, it is also revealed that this personal deity dwells as a Trinity of persons.[23] This is the central mystery of revealed religion, and it stands as the source for all other revelation.[24] God is a Trinity of persons. The Athanasian Creed testifies to this truth:

> Now this is the Catholic faith: We worship one God in the Trinity and the Trinity in unity, without either confusing the persons or dividing the substance; for the person of the Father is one, the Son's is another, the Holy Spirit's another; but the Godhead of the Father, Son, and Holy Spirit is one, their glory equal, their majesty coeternal.[25]

Why is this mystery important? How can this mystery assist humanity in understanding personhood and the related areas of autonomy, relationship, and love itself?

The Holy Trinity: Distinct and Relational

As revealed, God exists as a Trinity. The three persons are equal in divinity and majesty. Each person is distinct and yet relational to the other persons. In truth, the divine persons hold their distinctive nature, their self-possession, only in terms of their relationship. Thus, God the Father is "Father" because he is Father to the Son and Spirit, and the Son is "Son" because he is Son to the Father and Spirit, and the Spirit is the Love between the Father and Son.[26] The very self-possession, the autonomy, of the persons within the Trinity is held

15

not as a remote sovereign self but as a gift that is given through self-donation to the other persons within the Godhead.[27] Autonomy, therefore, should be seen as a person's distinctiveness that is summoned and fulfilled by self-donation within a community. This is a truth that must be constantly rediscovered and re-appreciated within humanity and its rapid technological advances.

Pope St. John Paul II would develop this understanding of autonomy and community. He taught that "God in his innermost essence is not solitude but family," and further in terms of human personhood, the great pontiff taught that "the person who does not give himself to another remains forever a juvenile."[28] Here the Holy Trinity, as the perfection of being and personhood, is understood in terms of relationship, communion, and family.

Infinitely perfect and blessed in himself, therefore, God chose to share the love he exchanged within his very self. The abundance of love that was held within the Triune community of persons overflowed into creation and was specifically offered to the human person. God was not a deity in need of our affirmation, worship, or submission. The love of God is an invitation to freedom and fulfillment, and humanity's desire to praise him adds nothing to his greatness but is itself a gift to humanity as it grows in its own understanding of personhood by a deeper realization of personal autonomy and self-donation.[29]

The human person, then, made in the image of this Triune God has a summons to this *ordo amoris*: to the call that sees one's self-possession as ordered to his self-donation, that sees one's autonomy within a broader context of service, responsibilities, and community.

"My God is Love"

In the plethora of stories surrounding Saint Teresa of Calcutta, there is one story that accentuates the self-donation within the divine persons of the Holy Trinity and the call of the human person to live this same spirit of service. Once, Mother Teresa was washing the body of a dying woman, who asked her why she was washing her. The woman was an untouchable in the Indian caste system and did not understand the act of kindness. Mother Teresa told the woman that she washed her because her God had sent her to the woman. But the woman told Mother Teresa that she was a Hindu and worshipped over four hundred gods. Which god did Mother represent? The woman told Mother that she did not know her God. Mother replied that she indeed knew her God. The woman again told Mother that she did not know her God and did not understand why she was with her and washing her. Mother Teresa gently answered the woman, "You know my God. My God is Love, and he has called me to be here with you."[30]

Mother Teresa modeled this first truth of the woman searching for the missing coin – namely, God searches for humanity in love.

Conclusion

In understanding the revealed truth about God and seeing the inner action of love within the Godhead, it is clear that the autonomy of the Divine Persons is an *ordo amoris*, an order of love. The Persons of the Godhead are distinct but their distinctiveness – their autonomy – is directed to the other persons and to self-donation.[31]

In this theological truth, humanity and specifically the medical community can see a rich and life-giving exposition of autonomy. Sometimes confused with a "self-will to power," or with notions of a sovereign self, autonomy can be used to isolate persons, objectify them, and manipulate their vanity or vulnerability. It can play on their fears of burden or blessing and cause harm to their dignity and the common good of the community in which they live and have rights and responsibilities. The human community needs a strong and balanced view of the autonomy of the human person as the Church shows how the love of God can temper, guide, and enrich the journey of life and the authentic flourishing of the person.

How did the living God demonstrate his self-donation for humanity itself? Is there a testimonial that gives credibility to the truth of autonomy and selfless service? What did God's search for humanity – flowing from his own inner life – look like in the course of history?

CHAPTER TWO

SERVICE AND THE MINISTRY OF JESUS CHRIST

Introduction

In order for humanity to fully understand human life, self-donation, suffering, and service to the sick and those in need, the Church looks to the ministry of Jesus Christ and draws principal lessons from him that can be instructive to anyone of good will.

The Light in the Darkness

As the woman searching for the coin lit a lamp, so God in his search for humanity lights a lamp. In the midst of the darkness, chosen and perpetuated by the fallen choices and sinful acts of humanity, God sent light.[32] The work of God within human history reached its climax when the Second Person of the Holy Trinity, God the Son, did not just bring light but came to humanity as the Light of the World.[33]

Why did he come? What did God the Son wish to accomplish? What lessons can this light teach humanity?

The Fall from Grace and Darkness

Christian theology recounts that humanity was created by God in a state of perfect justice marked by a harmony: between the person's soul and body, among human persons in community, and between

19

humanity and the rest of the created world. Within the human person, the soul held mastery over the body, and both the body and soul shared an inheritance of eternal life.[34]

The first human persons, called Adam and Eve, were given this blessed state and were told not to eat the fruit of the Tree of the Knowledge of Good and evil.[35] This directive was to show humanity its need for God and its responsibility to acknowledge God as both its Creator as well as the Author of the laws that govern all things, including the moral law of right and wrong.[36] The parents of humanity, however, chose to rebel against their loving Creator and chose a path contrary to the one indicated by him.[37] Adam and Eve abused the freedom that was given to them to love God by choosing a love of self, and they introduced discord between themselves and God, within their own personhood, between each other, and with the world around them.[38] As the Second Vatican Council teaches:

> Although he was made by God in a state of holiness, from the very onset of his history man abused his liberty, at the urging of the Evil One. Man set himself against God and sought to attain his goal apart from God. Although they knew God, they did not glorify Him as God, but their senseless minds were darkened and they served the creature rather than the Creator.

And the Council continues:

> Often refusing to acknowledge God as his beginning, man has disrupted also his proper relationship to his own ultimate goal as well as his whole relationship toward himself and others and all created things.[39]

Knowledge of Good and Evil

It should be clarified that the "figurative language"[40] that represented

20

a prohibition against eating of the Tree of the Knowledge of Good and Evil was not against a simple awareness of good and evil.[41] In fact, human persons are to actively question and seek to know what is good and what is evil. This is one of the powers given to humanity by our reason and one of the specific tasks of humanity.[42]

The exploration for such moral awareness is esteemed by the Church and by the Western intellectual tradition.[43] Delphi reminded its visitors, "Know yourself," and Socrates taught, "The unexamined life is not worth living." At the core of the axial revolution of the fifth century BC, which gave birth to Confucianism and Buddhism as well as Greek philosophy, was the very human search for life's meaning through moral questions about what is right and what is wrong.[44]

The prohibition, therefore, given by God was against a willed attempt to legislate and determine what is right and wrong for oneself. It was the renunciation of the sovereign self, seeing itself as the only source of law, removing itself from God, community, and the world, and then deciding in its own isolation what is right and wrong.[45]

Consequences of the Fall

As a consequence of the disobedience of humanity's first parents, human nature itself and all creation fell from grace.[46] Humanity created distorted images of God and presented him as an angry, vengeful deity seeking punishment and destruction. Humanity came to fear God and sought to hide from or rebel against him, and the moral law was falsely seen in terms of an external imposition upon the human person and a means of raw divine control.[47] Consequently, the fallen human mind and heart began to distrust God and notions of absolute truth. It began to doubt concepts such as "truth," "good" and "evil," and questioned the human person's capacity for goodness.[48]

The soul lost its own internal harmony and the mastery it held over the body. And while created good, the human person would now have an inclination toward evil and darkness.[49] Consequently, human persons were now inclined to their own comfort or interests over those of their neighbors, and humanity saw the world as a means of conquest and profit rather than a place calling for care and stewardship. The ability to believe and discern moral goodness through the natural light of reason would become more difficult and strenuous for humanity.[50]

Suffering and Illness

With the soul's mastery over the body lost, the human body would now experience death. The human person would suffer the plight of having an immortal soul within a mortal body. And with the loss of beatitude and the immortality of the body, suffering and illness became a part of human life.[51] As Pope John Paul II taught in his Apostolic Letter *Salvifici Doloris*:

> Man suffers on account of evil, which is a certain lack, limitation or distortion of good. We could say that man suffers because of a good in which he does not share, from which in a certain sense he is cut off, or of which he has deprived himself. He particularly suffers when he "ought"— in the normal order of things—to have a share in this good and does not have it.[52]

Christian belief, therefore, sees suffering and illness within the theological context of the Fall from grace and acknowledges them as evils within human life. They are not seen as the consequences of the actual sins of any one person after the Fall, but as a dark inheritance from the original sin of our first parents and the subsequent Fall within human nature itself.[53] From the Fall, human history will

22

include the sorrow and drama of illness and suffering.[54] The human story is marked by questions about evil, inquiries about suffering, debates over human dignity and quality of life, medical battles against illness and the care of the sick, and struggles with faith and understanding about moral goodness and responsibility. For the Christian believer and the discerning person of good will, answers to these questions begin with the Fall and its source as the cause of suffering and illness in human life.[55]

Do these evils have the last word in the human experience? Is there possibly a deeper understanding of suffering available to the human family?

Light of the World

In the fallenness of humanity, God the Son came as the Light of the World. As expressed by Pope John Paul II in his encyclical *Fides et Ratio*:

> In the Incarnation of the Son of God we see forged the enduring and definitive synthesis which the human mind of itself could not even have imagined: the Eternal enters time, the Whole lies hidden in the part, God takes on a human face.[56]

When the Son of God came, was it as a removed figure falling from the skies? Was he born from the mind of his divine father or from a peculiar sexual encounter as was commonly said of divinities within the myths of Greece and Rome? Was the Son of God a ghost or a theophany of some sort that merely appeared to be human? No, the Second Person of the Holy Trinity came as a human being. As St. Paul taught:

> But when the time had fully come, God sent forth his Son,

23

born of woman, born under the law, to redeem those who were under the law, so that we might receive adoption as sons.[57]

The divine Son became a full human being and experienced all things truly human.[58] He showed humanity its dignity as the children of God and taught the human family how it is to live. The Second Vatican Council instructed:

> For, by His incarnation, he, the Son of God, has in a certain way united Himself with each man. He worked with human hands, He thought with a human mind. He acted with a human will and with a human heart he loved.[59]

The Second Person of the Holy Trinity took on human flesh in Jesus of Nazareth.[60] He came as the fullness of all God's revelation. In summary, all that humanity had discerned of God through the light of natural reason and all that was supernaturally revealed to humanity about God was recapitulated and fulfilled in Jesus Christ.[61]

Humanity fell from grace by turning away from its loving Creator, and was on a path away from truth, beauty, and goodness. The Lord Jesus, fulfilling the prophetic call exemplified in God's encounter with the Prophet Isaiah: "Whom shall I send?" "Here I am, Lord, send me!" – freely chose to come and save what was lost.[62] He came as Light and entered into the darkness of the world.[63]

What was Jesus Christ's work within the human family? How is his ministry to be understood? What was the light he brought to humanity? How can the human family benefit from his saving work and witness?

The Savior of Humanity

While fully human, the Second Person of the Holy Trinity came as the long-awaited Savior. He was declared so at Caesarea-Philippi when St. Peter announced: "You are the Christ, the Son of the living God."[64]

Although fully human, and coming as the Savior of humanity, the Second Person of the Trinity did not lose his divinity. Jesus Christ was truly God and truly man. The Church would wrestle for centuries to understand this mystery. And, four centuries after St. Peter's confession at Caesarea-Philippi, the Church was in a position to give a full theological explanation of the God-Man. Pope St. Leo the Great drafted this explanation in his *Tome*, and the Council Fathers of Chalcedon accepted it. After the council accepted the *Tome*, they declared: "Peter has spoken through Leo."[65] The council summarized the Tome in its own declaration on Jesus Christ, and the truth that Jesus Christ is both God and Man is of high importance in understanding the help and direction his life and ministry can be to the human family. The council declared:

> Following the saintly fathers, we all with one voice teach the confession of one and the same Son, Our Lord Jesus Christ: the same perfect in divinity and perfect in humanity, the same truly God and truly man, of a rational soul and a body; consubstantial with us as regards his humanity; like us in all respects except for sin; begotten before the ages from the Father as regards his divinity, and in the last days the same for us and for our salvation from Mary, the virgin God-bearer, as regards his humanity; one and the same Christ, Son, Lord, only-begotten, acknowledged in two natures which undergo no confusion, no change, no division, no separation...

The council continued:

> ... at no point was the difference between the natures taken away through the union, but rather the property of both natures is preserved and comes together into a single person and a single subsistent being; he is not parted or divided into two persons, but is one and the same only-begotten Son, God, Word, Lord Jesus Christ, just as the prophets taught from the beginning about him, and as the Lord Jesus Christ himself instructed us, and as the creed of the fathers handed it down to us.[66]

The teachings of the Council of Chalcedon show that in every way Jesus of Nazareth was fully God and fully human without change, division or confusion.[67]

Why is the hypostatic union of Jesus Christ important? Why does his human nature play such a predominant role in understanding his saving work? What significance does this reality have for humanity?

Fully Human and Privation of Being

Jesus Christ is true God and true Man. As such, he is the model of what it means to be human.[68] In his life and work, the Lord Jesus showed humanity how to live and serve others. The Second Vatican Council taught:

> In reality it is only in the mystery of the Word made flesh that the mystery of man truly becomes clear. For Adam, the first man, was a type of him who was to come, Christ the Lord, Christ the new Adam, in the very revelation of the mystery of the Father and of his love, fully reveals man to himself and brings to light his most high calling.[69]

The reality of Jesus Christ revealing humanity to itself is exemplified by the poet Dante, who in his masterpiece *The Divine Comedy* revealed the face of God in this way:

> Within the profound and clear subsistence of the lofty Light appeared to me three circles of three colors and of one dimension; and one seemed reflected by the other, as Iris by Iris, and the third seemed fire which from the one and from the other is equally breathed forth. O Light Eternal, that sole abidest in Thyself, sole understandest Thyself, and, by Thyself understood and understanding, lovest and smilest on Thyself! That circle, which appeared in Three generated as a reflected light, being awhile surveyed by my eyes, seemed to me depicted with our effigy within itself, of its own very color; wherefore my sight was wholly set upon it.[70]

In this great poem, Dante sees a human likeness within the Godhead. The poet is stressing the point that Jesus Christ is a human being and that he discloses humanity to itself. By understanding the human identity of Jesus Christ, human persons can see a brighter reflection of humanity and thus can better and more deeply hear and appreciate the Lord's teachings and witness among us.[71]

The Lord Jesus does not teach as an outsider but as a human being, as someone within the human family.[72] In comprehending Jesus in this way, humanity can more deeply understand its own goodness and dignity. The human person's own identity as someone – not a *something* – with an incommunicable dimension that is made for self-donation and community life can be seen with clearer eyes in Jesus Christ.[73] Both of these truths are reflected in the mystery of the Holy Trinity and in the ministry of the Lord Jesus.

But what about the fallenness of humanity? Do not the sins of humanity prove it cannot follow the example given by Jesus? Does not sin show that humanity is only motivated by ambition and the desire for pleasure? How is sin to be understood in light of the ministry of Jesus Christ?

As humanity can see its fallenness: from concentration camps and killing fields, to racism and religious extremism, to the abuse of medicine or the neglect of those who are suffering, we can easily believe that human persons are evil. Such a conclusion about humanity, left to itself, would be understandable (even if wrong). Sin, however, has always been understood as a privation of being. In seeing that the world and the human person are good and have a natural orientation to goodness (although heavily influenced by an impulse to evil), sin is seen as a privation – a lacking or removal of being – and something that takes away goodness.[74]

In seeing sin as a privation, we understand that sin and evil are not portions of creation and humanity. When, therefore, it is said that Jesus Christ was fully human and yet lacking in sin,[75] it reflects the reality that sin is not human or real, but is actually anti-human and anti-reality. Sin, therefore, does not have the power to define humanity, even as it takes away the richness of the human essence and veils the goodness of the person and of creation, covering them with darkness.[76]

As the exemplar of humanity, Jesus Christ is without sin and he shows us how to live as fully human beings.[77] As the Savior of humanity, and the source of reconciliation between God and Man, Jesus takes away the sins of humanity allowing the person to be free to live out his inheritance as a person and a child of God.[78] Humanity, therefore, is defined by goodness and love. As Pope St. John Paul II declared: "We are not the sum of our weaknesses and failures. We are the sum of the Father's love for us and our real capacity to become the image of his Son."[79]

If the Lord Jesus did not sin or experience sin, how can he be the exemplar of humanity? How can someone without sin attempt to understand human life that has been marred by sin and guilt? What credibility does Jesus Christ have to humanity?

The Capacity to Suffer

Again, in trying to understand sin, it must be placed within its proper conclusion as a privation of being. Humanity cannot allow itself to be defined by sin, which is a privation of goodness, or to allow sin to become a standard of maturation or wisdom. As one popular American singer, formerly known as an advocate for pre-marital abstinence, recently declared in reference to his new promiscuous life, "I'm an adult in all ways."[80] This is a belief that runs contrary to rudimentary anthropology, principles of which grasp a broader understanding of the human person, as well as standards for maturity and adulthood. The human person is defined by goodness and virtue, and human maturity is given by love and through self-donation (and not merely through the sinful use of one's sexual powers).[81]

With this emphasis made however, sin and guilt do weigh heavily in the experiences of human life. How then, can the life and teachings of Jesus Christ help humanity? If Jesus is without sin, can he understand humanity and its struggles? How can Jesus' self-donation be appreciated and imitated within the human experience? In the end, what credibility does Jesus Christ legitimately have toward humanity?

In the early Church, the bishop Apollinarius denied that Jesus Christ had a rational human soul within his human nature. He argued that the divine nature fulfilled the person of Christ and so no human soul was needed. The Church, however, denounced such a view. The Lord

29

Jesus, it was argued, held a fully human nature, with a rational human soul. This is a very important truth in light of the significant powers of the human soul.[82]

In teaching that Jesus Christ had a human soul, the Church acknowledges that he had a capacity to suffer and feel pain. Without a human soul, this experience would not have been possible. And so, when it is said that the Lord Jesus had no sin, it does not mean that he did not experience sin and its consequences in our world. As seen throughout the account of his life in the Gospels, we see that the Lord Jesus did experience mourning, tiredness, righteous anger, loss, distress, anxiety, agony, fear of death and suffering, as well as other emotions and states within the human soul.[83] Jesus Christ knows every experience and has felt every emotion of one who is suffering, as well as the empathy and compassion of the loved ones of those who are ill or suffering.[84]

Does Jesus, however, only remain in the spiritual and emotional aspects of suffering? What does Jesus Christ do with his knowledge and experience of human life and suffering? What example does he present to all people of good will?

Salvation Through Suffering

No discussion of human life would be complete without addressing the full array of suffering, not only within the soul but also in the body.[85] In experiencing the fullness of human life, Jesus Christ understood and accepted all forms of suffering, and he desires to teach humanity the scope and truths surrounding human suffering.[86]

From the time of humanity's fall from grace, suffering has been an evil within human life. Christian theology has always seen suffering as an evil and as a consequence of the original sin of Adam and Eve. In taking on our human nature, Jesus Christ accepted the suffering of humanity, body and soul.[87] It is clearly seen, from his life of poverty, to living as a refugee in a foreign land, to being hunted down as a criminal, to the frustration of learning a trade, to the death of his foster father, to his experience of being tired and thirsty, as well as misunderstood, rejected, and unloved. All of his sufferings culminated in the cruelty and torture of his Passion, and the humiliation and asphyxiation of his Death. In all these sufferings, Jesus chose to accept, enter, and use suffering, which has been such a pivotal dilemma and source of anguish in human history, as the very means to manifest his love and self-donation for humanity. Suffering itself would become the instrument of salvation.[88] How is this possible? How did Jesus Christ use suffering for the redemption and renewal of humanity?

In taking on human suffering, the Lord Jesus went directly to sin, understood as the source of suffering in human life. In order to take away sin and vanquish its control on humanity, Jesus Christ became sin itself.[89] He sought to destroy this privation of being, and its consequences of suffering and death, from the inside out.[90] In becoming sin, Jesus took upon himself all the sins of humanity throughout time. He endured the totality of human guilt, shame, alienation, grief, confusion, and the full panorama of darkness caused by sin. As Pope John Paul II taught in his Encyclical *Dives in Misericordia:*

> The cross of Christ on Calvary is also a witness to the strength of evil against the very Son of God, against the one who, alone among all the sons of men, was by His nature absolutely innocent and free from sin, and whose coming into the world was untainted by the disobedience of Adam and the inheritance of original sin. And here, precisely in Him, in

31

Christ, justice is done to sin at the price of His sacrifice, of His obedience "even to death." He who was without sin, "God made him sin for our sake." Justice is also brought to bear upon death, which from the beginning of man's history had been allied to sin. Death has justice done to it at the price of the death of the one who was without sin and who alone was able-by means of his own death-to inflict death upon death. In this way the cross of Christ, on which the Son, consubstantial with the Father, renders full justice to God, is also a radical revelation of mercy, or rather of the love that goes against what constitutes the very root of evil in the history of man: against sin and death.[91]

The crucible for this radically human endeavor was the Lord's Passion, which began in the Garden of Gethsemane.[92] In the garden, as he took upon himself the sins of humanity, the Lord Jesus sweated blood, felt the full isolation caused by sin, and could not raise his eyes to the heavens.[93] In this sacrificial moment, the words of the Prodigal Son could be placed in the mouth of Jesus Christ as he suffered in the Garden: "Father, I have sinned against heaven and against you, and I am no longer worthy to be called your son."[94]

In the Garden of Gethsemane and by the full weight of his Passion, Death, and Resurrection, Jesus Christ proved his association with suffering humanity and began his Passion which destroyed the power of sin and death.[95] The suffering of the righteous man was foretold by the Prophet Isaiah in the Hebrew Scriptures:

> He was despised and rejected by men; a man of sorrows, and acquainted with grief; and as one from whom men hide their faces he was despised, and we esteemed him not.
>
> Surely he has borne our griefs and carried our sorrows; yet we

esteemed him stricken, smitten by God, and afflicted. But he was wounded for our transgressions, he was bruised for our iniquities; upon him was the chastisement that made us whole, and with his stripes we are healed. All we like sheep have gone astray; we have turned every one to his own way; and the Lord has laid on him the iniquity of us all.[96]

Even among people of good will, the suffering of the righteous is seen as a cause and source of hope and goodness. As Plato recorded the similar sufferings of the just man in a conversation between Socrates and Glaucon:

"As much as I can," he said. "With two such men [just and unjust] it's no longer hard, I suppose, to complete the speech by a description of the kind of life that awaits each. It must be told, then. And if it's somewhat rustically told, don't suppose that it is I who speak, Socrates, but rather those who praise injustice ahead of justice. They'll say that the just man who has such a disposition will be whipped; he'll be racked; he'll be bound; he'll have both his eyes burned out; and, at the end, when he has undergone every sort of evil, he'll be crucified and know that one shouldn't wish to be, but to seem to be, just.[97]

On account therefore of the unique depth of his human experience, Jesus Christ – true God and true Man – has complete credibility as the exemplar of what it means to be human. Additionally, his singular experiential knowledge of suffering in soul and body makes him the standard by which both the care of the sick and suffering can be evaluated and its moral discernment measured.

If Jesus Christ, however, has destroyed sin, why do illness and suffering still afflict humanity? How is humanity to understand suffering in light of the ministry of Jesus Christ?

Redemptive Suffering

While the ministry of Jesus Christ has destroyed the kingdom of sin and death, the consequences of sin still remain in the human experience. The difference, however, is that suffering – while an evil caused by original sin – can now become redemptive for the person and the community.[98] Rather than seeing suffering in merely negative terms, the example and ministry of Jesus now show the human family a positive way in which suffering can be seen and accepted in human life.[99]

Now, in Jesus Christ, suffering can be a source of repentance, purification, goodness, penance, renewal, hope and empathy for others who are sick or suffering in some way. In the Lord Jesus, who offered his sufferings as a self-oblation and as a means of selfless service, humanity can see suffering as a new way of service to others and as a new means of self-donation and salvation for themselves and the whole world. As the social commentator Malcolm Muggeridge wrote:

> Contrary to what might be expected, I look back on experiences that at that time seemed especially desolating and painful. I now look back upon them with particular satisfaction. Indeed, I can say with complete truthfulness that everything I have learned in my seventy-five years in this world, everything that has truly enhanced and enlightened my existence has been through affliction and not through happiness whether pursued or attained. In other words, I say this, if it were possible to eliminate affliction from our earthly existence by means of some drug or other medical mumbo-jumbo, the results would not be to make life delectable, but to

make it too banal and trivial to be endurable. This, of course, is what the cross signifies and it is the cross, more than anything else, that has called me inexorably to Christ.[100]

"I Am Jesus of Teresa"

Once, while St. Teresa of Avila was in prayer, the Lord Jesus appeared to her and asked her who she was. The saint replied with her Religious name, "I am Teresa of Jesus." The Lord smiled and when the saint asked him who he was, he replied to her, "I am Jesus of Teresa."[101]

This story illustrates the intimacy that Jesus Christ has with humanity. It shows that similar to the woman who lit a lamp searching for the missing coin, the Lord Jesus seeks out humanity. In this effort, Jesus Christ stands as an exemplar of what it means to be a human being and he shows the human family how to live as the children of God. While the witness of the righteous man was shown to the Prophets, it was discerned by the ancient Greeks just as it can be discerned today by people of good will. Truly this witness stands as a model of self-donation and self-service to others.

Conclusion

The Lord's example and ministry are for all people, of every time and place, each gender, every culture and socioeconomic status, and every profession and occupation, a light and an encouragement to moral goodness and service to the common good. In particular, due to its unique care of the sick and suffering, the life and teachings of Jesus Christ are of paramount importance to humanity.

For humanity to fully understand its gift of life, self-donation, suffering, and service to the sick and those in need, it must draw principal lessons from the life and ministry of Jesus.

CHAPTER THREE

VIRTUE AND THE CALL TO DISCIPLESHIP

Introduction

The Church draws various lessons from the call to discipleship given by the Lord Jesus. These lessons of freedom and virtue can be of help to anyone of good will. They serve as indications and as a template for healthy and happy living. The life of the person who has chosen to follow the Lord Jesus as one of his disciples should be a witness to true freedom and inspire strong virtue in all people of good will.

The Summons to Follow

Throughout the Gospel accounts, the Lord Jesus imitated the woman searching for the missing coin by sweeping the household of faith of false views of freedom, virtue, and discipleship.[102] He called humanity back to goodness and holiness,[103] and in his public ministry he constantly invited members of "the crowds" to follow him.[104] They witnessed his powerful preaching and wondrous signs and were invited to say "yes" to his summons and to acknowledge him as Lord and Savior.[105]

Only a few chose to accept the call, but for those who did, it made every difference in the way they lived, loved, forgave, hoped, and served. Pope St. John Paul II summarized the full response of the Christian disciple in this way:

The man who wishes to understand himself thoroughly – and not just in accordance with immediate, partial, often superficial, and even illusory standards and measures of his being – he must with his unrest, uncertainty, and even his weakness and sinfulness, with his life and death, draw near to Christ. He must, so to speak, enter into him with all his own self, he must 'appropriate' and assimilate the whole reality of the Incarnation and Redemption in order to find himself.

Within the person who responds in this way, the saintly pope continued:

If this profound process takes place within him, he then bears fruit not only of adoration of God but also of deep wonder at himself.[106]

As a person responds in faith to the invitation given by the Lord Jesus, he begins to be able to see the splendor of his own personhood and his vocation as a Christian disciple. Divine grace is able to work more deeply within him.[107] A radical change occurs by this awareness, an interior process that St. Paul calls "a new creation."[108] As the believer begins to "hunger and thirst for righteousness" this transformation happens more deeply. Again, Pope St. John Paul II teaches:

Faith is a decision involving one's whole existence. It is an encounter, a dialogue, a communion of love and life between the believer and Jesus Christ, the Way, the Truth, and the Life (cf. John 14:6). It entails an act of trusting abandonment to Christ, which enables us to live as he lived (cf. Galatians 2:20), in profound love of God and of our brothers and sisters.[109]

This process is not easy or comfortable for the disciple. It requires a constant conversion – a change – within the person and his worldview. As Pope St. John Paul II would emphasize:

From the outset, conversion is expressed in faith which is total and radical, and which neither limits nor hinders God's gift. At the same time, it gives rise to a dynamic and lifelong process which demands a continual turning away from "life according to the flesh" to "life according to the Spirit" (cf. Romans 8:3-13). Conversion means accepting, by a personal decision, the saving sovereignty of Christ and becoming his disciple.[110]

Why is this conversion important? Is it merely spiritual or are there tangible indications of it in our world today? How could the life of the Christian believer serve as a model and inspiration to all people of good will? How could this witness help the human family in more deeply understanding its call to service and community?

Personal Relationship

The Christian believer experiences this conversion precisely because of his response in faith to Jesus Christ. As Pope Benedict XVI taught:

> Being a Christian is not the result of an ethical decision or a lofty idea, but the encounter with an event, a person, which gives life a new horizon and a decisive direction.[111]

The conversion of the Christian, therefore, is a result of his choosing to enter into a personal relationship with Jesus Christ in the midst of the community of faith.[112] The way of life of the believer is an expression and a living out of the relationship he has with Jesus Christ. This way of life is ennobled by grace and elevated by the working of the Holy Spirit.[113]

Every Christian virtue, however, has a natural parallel that can be valued and exercised by any person of good will.[114] The Christian is called to model and demonstrate virtue, as a reflection of his love for

God and neighbor, as well as to give a lived testimony to holiness and humanity's capacity for goodness.[115] As Pope John Paul II taught:

> Since Christians are re-clothed in Christ Jesus and refreshed by his Spirit, they are "holy". They therefore have the ability to manifest this holiness and the responsibility to bear witness to it in all that they do. The apostle Paul never tires of admonishing all Christians to live "as is fitting among saints" (Eph. 5:3). Life according to the Spirit, whose fruit is holiness (cf. Rom 6:22; Gal 5:22), stirs up every baptized person and requires each to follow and imitate Jesus Christ, in embracing the Beatitudes... in family or in community, in the hunger and thirst for justice, in the practice of the commandment of love in all circumstances of life and service to the brethren, especially the least, the poor and the suffering.[116]

How does virtue develop in the human person? What is the role of the moral law in forming virtue? What role does freedom play in the person's desire for virtue and goodness?

Freedom, the Moral Law, and Virtue

The moral law is a gift given by God. It helps to order our fallen nature and prepare us for virtue.[117] While human persons were created good, as children of Adam and Eve they have a fallen nature and a disordered attraction to evil and waywardness. At times, the person can create a law according to his own flesh – the flesh being an inordinate desire for evil, and not necessarily a synonym for our body – and he can allow himself to be ruled by a false law.[118] The person can rationalize and justify all kinds of evil, and even call good things evil and evil things good.[119] In light of this inclination, humanity needs help. It needs instruction. God's moral law is written on the human heart and is discernible within the consciences of all people of good will.[120] It is humanity's pedagogue, its tutor, which shows the human family the right path to live according to human nature and sound reason.[121]

The moral law teaches humanity right from wrong, accuses it of its wicked actions, and denounces it in its waywardness. The moral law is a demanding tutor. It cannot heal or save humanity, but it is meant to instruct and educate. Before humanity can begin to desire virtue, it must first allow God's law to teach and admonish it. By showing humanity its sin, the moral law enables the human family to see the virtue that is offended by its sin.[122] In life, therefore, a human person can juggle the accusation of the law on one hand and his desire for virtue on the other.

As the moral law teaches humanity, it prepares it for true freedom.[123] Freedom is often poorly defined as an ability to do whatever is wanted, but freedom is actually the ability to do what is right.[124] Due to its fallenness, if humanity were left to its own devices, it would choose sin and not enjoy freedom. Freedom, therefore, is an openness to God (however he might be understood) that allows the Holy Spirit to work within the person's interior life.[125] Freedom is a maturity of the soul that empowers the person to act above his passions and desires, to see the proper order of things, and to do what is right.[126]

The human person has to grow into his freedom and safeguard it so that his freedom itself does not become enslaved. St. Paul summarizes these truths when he writes: "For freedom Christ has set us free; stand fast therefore, and do not submit again to a yoke of slavery."[127] And again, the Apostle writes: "Now the Lord is the Spirit, and where the Spirit of the Lord is, there is freedom."[128] This understanding of freedom from St. Paul helps to highlight the proper relationship between the moral law and freedom. Oftentimes, the moral law and freedom are falsely portrayed as being in contradiction, as if the two are in tension with one versus the other.[129] The reality, however, is that there is no "versus" between the moral law and freedom, but rather a rapport of *via*, meaning "by way of," which demonstrates that the law is in service to freedom and freedom benefits from the discipline of the law. The law helps the person to be free.[130] The person therefore who repeatedly breaks the moral law lives a life according to his passions and desires. The person's freedom is enslaved. He is not free. For the person to mature fully, he needs both the law and freedom, and together they pave the way for a virtuous life.[131]

Virtue is best understood, therefore, as a good habit that governs human action, orders its passions, and guides its conduct according to faith and reason. It is the power to make the right choice, at the right time, in the right situation. As the law secures freedom, so the law and freedom become the means for grace to ennoble the person to exercise virtue.[132] Examples of virtues include faith, hope and love,[133] as well as prudence, justice, temperance, and fortitude.[134] Other virtues include patience, compassion, gentleness, self-control, and generosity. For the Christian believer, virtue is the Lord's daily call that tells him what to do in his life. There is nothing more tangible and practical in this world than holiness. Virtue is more real than the physical objects of the world, and it shows the world holiness. It helps the human family to see, hear, taste, smell, and touch God's presence among us.[135]

The person of good will, who perhaps has no religious faith, can aspire to freedom and the process of exercising natural virtue in his own interior life.[136] The natural virtues, upon which the Christian virtues flourish, are available and justly expected of every civil person by their spouse, family, society, culture, and professional association.

For example, the Christian witness can be of supreme help to the medical professional as he tries to live up to this call for virtue and goodness.

Jesus Christ is Lord

In the years after Jesus' death and Resurrection, Saul of Tarsus was a fierce persecutor of the Christian community and a man who was feared by believers: "Saul laid waste to the Church, entered house after house, dragged off men and women and committed them to prison."[137] After persecuting the Church in Jerusalem, Saul was "still breathing threats and murder against the disciples of the Lord" and asked for letters to go to Damascus and search for any Christians.[138] On his way to the city, "a light from heaven flashed about him," and a voice said to him, "Saul, Saul, why do you persecute me?" When Saul asked who it was, the voice responded, "I am Jesus, whom you are persecuting."[139] After this encounter with the Lord, Saul was blinded and did not eat for three days.

This experience led to Saul's conversion to Jesus Christ. After accepting the graces of conversion, he realized that he needed to change his life. He spent three years in the desert of Arabia,[140] and later sought instruction from St. Peter and the other apostles.[141] Saul's conversion made him a different person, so much so that he decided to change his name in a sense and be called exclusively by his Roman name, "Paul."[142] And St. Paul would declare "Jesus Christ is Lord,"[143] and give testimony to his conversion:

> I have been crucified with Christ, it is no longer I who live, but Christ who lives in me; and the life I now live in the flesh I live by faith in the Son of God, who loved me and gave himself for me.[144]

The conversion in Saul's life led him to leave vice and darkness behind him, especially violence and intolerance. He became a better person in becoming a Christian. Thus, St. Paul is an example to others who might lean towards violence, struggle with intolerance, or suffer from some other sinful inclination. This exemplifies the power of the Christian witness in the world today.

Conclusion

The Church draws various lessons from the Lord Jesus who, like the woman looking for the lost coin, sweeps a house in search for something invaluable. The Lord seeks to sweep the household of faith (and the world) of vice and a slavery to darkness. These lessons of freedom and virtue, therefore, can guide and direct anyone of good will. They can serve as sources of education and as an outline for healthy and happy living. The life of the person who chooses to follow the Lord Jesus as one of his disciples, like Saint Paul, should be a witness to true freedom and inspire strong virtue in all people of good will.

CHAPTER FOUR

THE ROLE OF A TEACHER AND THE SHEPHERDS OF THE CHURCH

Introduction

The Church serves the People of God as shepherd, priest, and teacher. Commissioned by the Lord Jesus, the magisterium seeks to teach the ways of God to the community of disciples. In addition, as a service to humanity, the Church engages the entire human family and seeks to teach moral truths that can assist all human persons to live an abundant life. In light of the weaknesses and various inclinations of reason left to itself, the Church is a guide to moral reasoning and an aide in interpreting the natural law.[145] The Church sees humanity as a friend, neighbor, a fellow servant to humanity, and a partner in dialogue that seeks moral truth, goodness, and authentically compassionate care of the sick and suffering.[146]

An Ordained Teaching Office

In calling together a community of disciples, the Lord Jesus established and commissioned a teaching office – a magisterium – consisting of St. Peter, the chief apostle, and a group of other chosen apostles that would lead, witness to, and teach the community.[147] The magisterium is like the woman who searched for her coin and, upon finding it, called together her neighbors. The

44

magisterium holds the community of faith together as a shepherd and teacher.[148]

While all disciples share in the mission entrusted to the Church in the midst of the world, the apostles – and the bishops, who are their successors throughout time – are the Christ-appointed shepherds of the Church.[149] Within the community of faith, there is an equality in dignity and activity among the various members since all members cooperate in building up the Church; however, the teaching office is needed in order to exemplify the Christian way of life as well as to assure the Church's unity and clarity of doctrine and mission.[150] And so, while the baptized disciples are called to live as priests, prophets, and kings in the midst of their secular duties, the bishops (and their co-workers, the presbyters) properly serve as priests, teachers, and shepherds within the household of faith, to the community of believers.[151]

In approaching the truths of faith, no one can proclaim the Gospel to himself, just as no one can give the evangelical mandate to himself. Every person must hear from someone else and be the recipient of the truths of faith.[152] The magisterium is the office established by the Lord Jesus that teaches and proclaims, protects and clarifies, applies and interprets, the truths contained in the deposit of faith.[153]

No pope or bishop takes this authority on himself, and no one administers it based solely on his own personality or intellectual ability.[154] This authority of the magisterium is the authority of Jesus Christ who is acknowledged and revered in faith by the community of disciples as both Savior and Lord.[155] The authority of the magisterium, therefore, is guided and animated by the Holy Spirit.[156] Even as the shepherds deal and battle with their own fallenness, weaknesses, and sinfulness, the authority that is exercised by them is from a teaching authority that is divinely instituted and divinely protected.[157]

The exercise of the magisterium, however, is not the single role of any one person. Not even the pope is called to exercise the magisterium alone. The teaching office has a collegial character. As with St. Peter and the Apostles, so with the pope and bishops: they are chosen together and sent together. The fraternal unity between the pope and bishops is the basis of the unity of the entire Church. The pope and bishops pray, reflect, debate, study, listen, and dialogue with one another as they discern truth and the deposit of faith seeking to understand and apply them in our world today.[158]

The magisterium exercises its authority not only in passing on orthodoxy – a right praise of God and by extension sound doctrine – but also by orthopraxy – a right living and doing good in imitation of Jesus Christ.[159] The magisterium, in following the Lord Jesus, both speaks and acts as a means of teaching the People of God.[160] This is why the Church, in living her divine call and imitating the Lord Jesus' care for humanity, runs schools, hospitals, outreach centers, and other health and human services.[161]

In light of how it is exercised, the specific mission of the magisterium is linked to the definitive nature of the covenant God made with humanity in Jesus Christ.[162] It is called and empowered, therefore, to preserve the deposit of faith from all deviations and defections as a pastoral duty to the People of God. The magisterium guarantees the true faith without error to all believers, and it exercises its authority as a means to help all the members of the Church to abide in truth and the way of life exemplified by the Lord Jesus.[163]

What does this authority look like within the Church?

Does the magisterium have a role outside of the Church? How is the magisterium supposed to be looked upon and approached by the broader human family?

Teaching Within the Household of Faith (*Ab Intra*)

The magisterium's commission to teach is directly related to the community of faith. For the Christian believer, the teaching office is an extension of Christ's own teaching. The two cannot be separated.[164]

For the believer, therefore, the response to the magisterium is understood within their discipleship. Rather than a removed oppressive authority, it is viewed as a portion of the very body to which the disciple belongs, and as a guide and source of wisdom and instruction. It is a welcomed teacher. In receiving the teachings of the magisterium, the disciple is called to hold the bond of unity in terms of doctrine, liturgy, and leadership.[165] The Church relies on the Christian disciple to give an "obedience of faith" to her doctrinal teachings.[166] This expectation, however, should not lead to a *fideism* that abandons reason or an *ultramontanism* that falsely gives the obedience of faith not solely to doctrine but to expressed prudential judgments or theological opinions of the magisterium. Such extremism does not help the magisterium in its pastoral duty to teach and guide.[167]

In expressing the deliberation and discernment of the magisterium, it is important to note that the teaching office is within the Church and is in the service to the People of God. The magisterium's teachings, guided by the Holy Spirit, are meant to help the disciple follow the Lord Jesus, live a holy and virtuous life, and reach eternal life with the Holy Trinity. The magisterium, therefore, listens to the faithful, observes the practice of the faith, and seeks to understand truth in light of this lived experience. The *sensus fide* (the sense of faith) relies on the *sensus fidelium* (the sense of the faithful), and there is a dynamic

47

rapport between the two as the magisterium seeks to teach both truth and goodness in Christ's name.[168]

Is teaching moral truth within the Church enough? Does the magisterium have a role to play outside of the Church? If so, what teaching role should the magisterium be given?

In Service to the Common Good (*Ad Extra*)

The magisterium of the Church does not suspend its teaching to those beyond the community of faith. Quite the opposite, since the magisterium has a clear understanding of human nature and the supernatural assurance of its moral teachings, it knows that its truths are immutable and immemorial.[169] It is confident that its teachings apply to all people regardless of religious association or no religious affiliation at all, and that they can form consciences and help nurture the common good.[170] The Church, therefore, has the great hope that all people of good will would welcome her teachings and be readily open to discuss and be in dialogue about them.[171]

While a supra spatial-time entity, the Church is also living in the here and now and is a part of the joys and sorrows of humanity.[172] As such, the Church seeks to be a good neighbor to all and to collaborate in the ongoing effort to know moral truth, foster goodness within the human family, enrich the common good, and serve the sick, suffering, and those in need within the human family.[173]

In its collaboration, as it teaches outside of the community of faith, the magisterium will adjust its mode of teaching and focus on the use of reason and philosophy.[174] The Church does this for several reasons. First, the magisterium recognizes the ability and capacity of human reason to discern moral truth. It also knows, however, that human reason can be weak or inclined to evil, and so she engages human reason presenting moral arguments and desiring to elevate reason to a higher level in which moral goodness is desired and discerned.[175] Additionally, the Church uses reason and philosophy in order to respect the views and beliefs of those within a pluralistic society, as well as to make as strong an argument as possible for the moral teachings it presents.[176] Moreover, the Church takes such a posture in order to provide a shared language, as much as possible, between herself and those outside of the community of faith.[177] This is a necessary point that needs to be made, especially in a pluralistic society.[178]

The Church makes these efforts because they involve the care and well-being of humanity, which are of significant importance as the Church attempts to live out the way of life modeled by Jesus Christ, especially among the sick and suffering. And so, the Church desires to be involved as a willing partner with any government, group, or human services system that authentically serves and helps those who are sick or in need of assistance. In addition to being a partner in doing such good work among the sick and those in need, the Church is also involved in this work as a Christian witness, an interpreter of natural law and a teacher of moral goodness to humanity and the medical community.[179]

Is this effort to teach moral truth by the magisterium only a veiled attempt to proselytize? What good does the Church seek? What does she gain by such an effort?

Not a Direct Work of Evangelization

While it is true that the Church's very heart is evangelization, there are times when the Church is involved in aspects of a pluralistic society and does not seek to directly evangelize.[180] This is especially the case when she is in service to the common good of society, such as in areas of education, social outreach, and healthcare. In such encounters, the Church lives and presents her own confessional institutions as well as her moral teachings within the public forum as a sign of her love and concern for humanity and as a sincere service and guide to it. In such moments, she is not necessarily engaging in direct evangelization but is a witness to love and a cooperator with her neighbors.[181] As the Second Vatican Council teaches:

But at the same time, the Church, sent to all peoples of every time and place... Faithful to her own tradition and at the same time conscious of her universal mission, she can enter into communion with the various civilizations, to their enrichment and the enrichment of the Church herself... By riches coming from above, it makes fruitful, as it were from within, the spiritual qualities and traditions of every people of every age. It strengthens, perfects and restores them in Christ. Thus, the Church, in the very fulfillment of her own function, stimulates and advances human and civic culture; by her action, also by her liturgy, she leads them toward interior liberty.[182]

In such scenarios, the Church is not necessarily presenting moral teachings with the specific goal or focus of winning converts to the Christian faith, rather her focus is to assist society in knowing and living by what is true, good, and beautiful.[183]

With this clarification given, admittedly there are times when some people are so moved by the moral teachings that are being witnessed to and lived, that they seek admission into the Church. Such was the case of Dr. Bernard Nathanson. The doctor was a leading abortion provider. He heard the moral arguments presented by many people (developed in large part by the Catholic Church) and was dismissive of them and even mocked them. Over time, however, moral truth began to bother him and eventually he stopped performing abortions, although he still argued for abortion rights. In time, the doctor found himself an opponent of abortion. Dr. Nathanson was so inspired by the Catholic Church in this whole process that he was formally received into the Catholic Church by Cardinal John O'Connor in 1996. At his death, he was hailed as one of the leading medical voices in the pro-life movement in the United States.[184] While such conversions are welcomed, and the Church rejoices over them, her involvement in the public forum in teaching moral truth does not necessarily have these conversions as her direct focus. The Church seeks to be a sincere voice and guide in a pluralistic culture's search for moral principles and a more just society.[185]

In her dialogue with the broader society, and specifically with the medical community, the Church is always true to her own confessional beliefs, while also teaching moral truth as a service to humanity and as a witness to moral goodness and service.[186] In these efforts, the Church seeks to always accompany and guide humanity in its discernment and exploration of truth, beauty, and goodness.[187]

Conclusion

As the magisterium of the Church fulfills its mission within the household of faith, she also engages the world with a presentation and teaching on moral truth. As Christian disciples receive the magisterium's instruction with the "obedience of faith," their example shows all people of good will the necessity of having a guide and teacher in trying to exercise their reason and discern right from wrong. Always a servant and witness, the magisterium – honoring and defending the religious liberty of all – seeks to share, present, and teach moral truth to all people of good will.

CHAPTER FIVE

THE NEED FOR COMMUNITY AND THE CHURCH OF JESUS CHRIST

Introduction

The magisterium of the Church looks at the community that the Lord Jesus has called together and draws certain truths from the ecclesial identity that can assist anyone of good will to understand the human need for community. In seeing the call for community within our human nature, the magisterium calls on all people of good will, to recognize their rights and responsibilities within a community. The Church upholds that each person has a role and a part to play in a community, and no one can grow or flourish in isolation.

The Ecclesial Identity

Guided by the Holy Spirit, Christian believers are led to an encounter with Jesus Christ, and then to make a personal decision for him. As believers declare that "Jesus Christ is Lord," they join a community of other believers who have also made this declaration.[188] Believers in Jesus Christ are never alone. Their discipleship always includes them within the community of faith.[189] Just as the woman who searched for her missing coin upon finding it, called together her friends and rejoiced, the Church in like manner, calls the household of faith together to rejoice and to celebrate the Eucharist. This is the basis of the Church's identity as a faith community and as a people of worship.[190]

In light of the Eucharist and the process of joining a community of faith, an important distinction has to be made. No person has an individual relationship with the Lord Jesus in the sense that "individual" means an esoteric "me and Jesus" rapport. Rather, every human being is called to have a personal relationship with the Lord Jesus in the midst of the community of faith, within the people to whom God is united by a covenant.[191] There is no "me and Jesus," but rather a "we and Jesus" in the life of faith. It is important that the difference between "individual" and "personal" is understood.[192] Though faith is a personal act – my commitment to Jesus Christ – it is not a relationship solely mine. The believer can say: "My faith truly depends on others, and the faith of others depends on my faith." Again, no believer walks alone, but each is united to one another by Baptism and their personal decision for Jesus Christ. This unity is fully expressed as the community comes together to celebrate the Eucharist.[193]

Heaven is Other People

The existentialist philosopher Sartre believed "hell is other people."[194] To the degree that the darkness and struggles of life can lead a person to such a fallen belief, the Christian believer responds with the communion of saints. The communion of saints is the mutual exchange of spiritual goods among the holy ones.[195]

The belief in the communion of saints begins here are on earth as all the baptized, the "holy ones," are united in liturgy, doctrine, and pastoral leadership.[196] This is reflected in the nave of St. Peter's Basilica in Rome – the sanctuary of St. Peter the Apostle and a universally recognized symbol of the Christian faith – where there are brass markers that record major cities throughout the world and from the different continents. The markers indicate the unity of all believers throughout the world, from every culture, language, society, and people. The baptized are brought together and held as one body by the bond of charity given by the Spirit.[197]

The communion of saints, however, is not seen as concluding with just the living "holy ones" on earth. The communion of saints also includes those who have passed from this life in the state of grace but are still in a time of purgation. The Lord continues his work of redemption on these souls of the Church Suffering.[198]

The crown of the communion of saints is the triumphant souls in heaven, who dwell with God forever in glory. This group includes everyone in heaven and is accentuated by the canonized saints of the Church.[199] The canonized saints are those souls placed on the canon of the Church for public veneration and emulation. These souls are specifically chosen as particular models of holiness, virtue, and of all the ways that mark the life of a child of God. The saints are viewed as the friends of God and the older brothers and sisters of the other members within the communion of saints.[200]

All believers throughout time, therefore, are members of the communion of saints to some degree. This is an important awareness of the disciple. For example, the married Christian medical doctor who cares for the terminally ill is (and sees himself as) a member of the vast supra-time and space community of virtue and holiness united in Jesus Christ.[201] He understands his vocation to holiness, to the Christian way of life, from the teaching of the magisterium, but also by the example of the holy ones within the communion of saints.[202]

The actions and life of the Christian are not private affairs, therefore, but are viewed within this community of holiness. The believer understands this communion of saints and the privilege and responsibility he holds by living within it. The believer's virtue and living out of his vocation, his love and service to others, and the completion of his duties in life are all a part of the building up of this communion.[203] The Christian disciple is called to be an active member and participate in this living communion of grace and holiness.

Eucharist as Summit and Source

The Eucharist is properly understood as the summit and source of the entire Christian life. Every good thing the believer does points to it, and from it the believer finds the strength to do all other good things.[204] In the Eucharist, a Greek word meaning "thanksgiving," the community of faith celebrates that the Lord has ransomed them, is saving them, and is present among them.[205]

The Lord Jesus promised that he would not leave humanity as an orphan,[206] and so he is present to the community of faith in their service to one another, in his shepherds, in the Sacred Scriptures, and most especially in the Eucharist.[207] In the celebration of the Eucharist, under the appearance of bread and wine, the Lord Jesus makes his dwelling among humanity.

The Eucharistic celebration lies at the very core of the Christian way of life.[208]

In the Eucharistic celebration, not only does the Lord Jesus come to humanity, but the believer is also invited to offer his own life in Jesus Christ to God the Father. As the sacrifice of Jesus is "re-presented" to the Father by the power of the Holy Spirit, the believer – called to communion – is to offer his own life with Jesus Christ. All of the believer's hopes, joys, sufferings, and work, along with his trials and triumphs, are to be offered to God.[209] This spiritual oblation manifests the service the believer is called to also give to God, to the faith community, and to all people of good will.[210] In the Eucharist, the believer is invited to celebrate and rejoice with his fellow believers in order to receive the strength and joy to live as a disciple of the Lord, who is present to him in the Eucharistic celebration. From this rejoicing, therefore, the believer intimately understands the importance of the community and his place within it.[211]

A Fellowship by Nature

The communion of saints of the Christian believers highlights an important aspect of human nature. The human person is called to be in community.[212] While it is difficult to discern or to fulfill this call within contemporary Western culture, defined by individualism and utilitarianism, the human person knows he needs other people. He feels this loss, anxiety, emptiness, and confusion when he does not have relationships with others.[213] The person is an amazing subsistent who is shaped and molded by his network of relationships and the matrix of his responsibilities and obligations. A person stands not simply as himself, but also as son, brother, friend, employee, patient, neighbor, parishioner, etc., and most broadly as fellow human being. The person knows himself, and the depth of his identity, by being in the twists and turns of life with others. No person can flourish by himself and no one can completely understand himself without others.[214] These are basic human truths that can be seen and accentuated in the Christian way of life and in the Eucharistic celebration.

The person's natural inclination to community also highlights several important aspects of social and moral life. As the person knows his call to family, friends, and society, he matures and more deeply comprehends his duties and responsibilities to others. He realizes that his life is not his own and that he must fulfill his duties and serve others. He understands that his decisions affect others (and vice versa) and that his autonomy is a self-possession that is given to him so that he has something to give others. It is not meant to be a bastion of individualism, but a means of self-donation.[215] This realization could be found in a young father who realizes the weight of parenthood and yet gives his all, or the medical doctor who sees his patient's fear and spends more time with her, or the single person who feels alone but serves the homeless and hungry within her community because she knows that human fellowship is more important than feelings of loneliness. The human person grows and develops and becomes more himself by his desire to be in community and to help others according to his own talents and position in society.[216]

One Equal to Anthony

In the early Church, the desert father Anthony was regarded as the holiest man alive. He was revered for his severe penances, depth of prayer, and divine wisdom. People would travel through the desert to spend a few minutes with him. He was hailed as a living saint. In the account of the Desert Fathers, however, there was one person who was regarded as an equal to Anthony. Surprisingly, the man was not a celibate or desert hermit. The man was a widower and medical doctor, who served his patients with compassion and kindness. He spent long hours with them and would not accept payment. In terms of devotion, every night he attentively prayed the *Sanctus* of the sacred liturgy. In these simple ways, by living within a community and seeking to serve others, he rivaled Anthony as the holiest man alive.[217] This is one example of a human person, a Christian believer, who understood the call to community and grew in virtue and holiness through it.

The Church, therefore, knows by faith and asserts that every person has a role and a part to play in a community, and no one can grow or flourish by himself. The human person needs others. Like the woman who searches for the missing coin, finds it, calls together her friends, and rejoices, so the Church, as a communion of saints and a reflection of what humanity is called to be, comes together as a community of faith and rejoices as one body as it worships the living God in the Eucharistic celebration.

CONCLUSION & CHALLENGE

The Church, therefore, as the community that has been called together by the Lord Jesus, reflects in her life certain truths that can assist anyone of good will to understand the human need for community and the call to service. In knowing the call for community within our human nature, the magisterium invokes all people of good will to recognize their rights and responsibilities within a community. This understanding of community is essential as the Church teaches and argues for the use of the natural moral law within the formation of consciences and the flourishing of the human family.

We rejoice in the realization that God is searching for us! We are invited to see the intricacies and depth of this search so as to recognize, know, and feel the tender love and attentive care the living God has for each of us.

We've taken a journey that has explored this pursuit by God. We have labored to understand God's search for each of us. In this walk, we've relied heavily on the Gospel story of the woman who lost a coin and searched for it, lit a lamp to help her look for it, swept her house feverishly, found the coin, invited her friends to come together, and then hosted a joyful celebration. Using the five-part division of the movement with the Gospel story, we dissected a parallel of these movements by highlighting and elucidating pressing theological truths.

In using the story, we addressed autonomy in terms of God's careful search for us. We emphasized service in the ministry of Jesus Christ by a reference to lighting a lamp and receiving enlightenment for the pursuit. Additionally, we elaborated on virtue and the call to discipleship as God's way of sweeping a house while looking for the lost coin. We described the role of a teacher by stressing the role of the shepherds of the Church, as guides in calling people together. Lastly, we explained the need for community and showed the Church of Jesus Christ as hosting a celebration and rejoicing on being found by God.

And so, we've developed these five essential theological truths — autonomy, service, virtue, the role of a teacher, and the need for community life — so as to display God's adamant search for each of us and for the entire human family in the course of the ages.

These truths, when appreciated and welcomed, can help us to not only see God's presence and pursuit of us but they can also show us the means and the way to surrender to this search and joyfully live as children of God.

To the degree that this fundamental belief of God's search for us is received and brought back to the heart of Western culture is the degree to which this culture, its institutions, and customs will regain their power and influence to shape and mold Western society in the recognition of human dignity, freedom, moral goodness, and a holistic and edifying common good. The aspiration for cultural reform is as tangible as the Incarnation of Jesus Christ, and the hope for cultural restoration and rejuvenation are as realistic as His Passion, Death, and Resurrection. The beliefs that created Western culture are the very beliefs that can renovate and enrich it. What will we do? Where will we turn?

With these truths to strengthen us, dear reader, we are called — each of us — to be witnesses of God's love and carriers of the truth to our culture. We are summoned to live these truths and let them shine as a light to the nations. We are commissioned to take these truths out into our world, to generously share them with others, and to unleash the power of truth that will transform lives and culture. This is our task. The harvest is abundant but the laborers are few.

ABOUT THE AUTHOR

Father Jeff Kirby is the Parish Priest of Our Lady of Grace Parish in Indian Land, South Carolina (gracewepray.org). He holds a doctorate in moral theology from the Holy Cross University in Rome and a Master of Arts in Philosophy from the Franciscan University of Steubenville. Father Kirby serves as an Adjunct Professor of Theology at Belmont Abbey College and Pontifex University. He has authored several books, including *Lord, Teach Us to Pray*, *Kingdom of Happiness: Living the Beatitudes in Everyday Life*, and most recently, *Be Not Troubled: A 6-Day Personal Retreat with Fr. Jean-Pierre DeCaussade*.

In 2016, Father Kirby was recognized by Governor Nikki Haley and granted the Order of the Palmetto, South Carolina's highest civilian honor, for his service to local communities and young adults throughout the state.

Working with St. Benedict Press and Catholic Scripture Study International, Father Kirby was the Host of the award-winning program Doors of Mercy and was one of the co-instructors of the programs, *Luke: The Gospel of Mercy and Jesus Revealed*.

Father Kirby is the weekly spirituality Contributor for the news site Crux: Taking the Catholic Pulse.

ENDNOTES

Introduction

[1] Abraham Joshua Heschel emphasized this point within the Jewish tradition in his book *God's Search for Man* (New York: Farrar, Straus, and Giroux, 1976). This truth is worth approaching from the Jewish perspective as it sets the stage for its radical fulfillment in the Incarnation.

[2] In similar fashion, and following his same style, Rabbi Heschel made the point as well in his book, *Man's Quest for God* (Santa Fe: Aurora Press, 1998). The quest to "find God" or to understand him on our own terms is developed by several scholars, especially John Courtney Murray, *The Problem of God* (Yale: University Press, 1965); Etienne Gilson, *The Unity of Philosophical Experience* (San Francisco: Ignatius Press, 1999); and Victor Frankl, *Man's Search for Meaning* (Boston: Beacon Press, 2006). Each of these scholars, using their own disciplines and methods, illustrate humanity's search to find and understand God. While such efforts are noble, in the end they have to accept the reality that before humanity looks for God, he has already been searching for it.

[3] Pope Benedict XVI, Mass for the Inauguration of the Pontificate (24 April 2005).

[4] Karol Wojtyla, *Love and Responsibility* (New York: Farrar, Straus, and Giroux, 1981), p. 41; cf. Pope John Paul II, Encyclical *Redemptor Hominis,* as found at vatican.va, John Paul II, Encyclicals (4 March 1979), #10.

[5] Pope John Paul II describes this action of the Holy Trinity in his Encyclical *Dives in Misericordia* (13 November 1980), #11-12, 58.

Chapter One

[6] Pope Benedict XVI, Encyclical *Caritas in Veritate,* #2.

[7] Cf. The teachings of the Fourth Lateran Council: "Between Creator and creature no similitude can be expressed without implying an even greater dissimilitude," as found in John Evans, *The Statutes of the Fourth General Council of the Lateran* (New York: Ulan Press, 2012). The apophatic understanding in theology and the spiritual life is explained well by Gregory Rocca, *Speaking the Incomprehensible God: Thomas Aquinas on the Interplay of Positive and Negative Theology* (Washington, DC: Catholic University of America Press, 2008), pp. 1-26, 27-48, and Denys Turner, *Darkness of God: Negativity in Christian Mysticism* (Cambridge: University Press, 1998), pp. 11-18, 50-74, 186-210. Both books describe this apophatic aspect of theology as a *via negativa* of knowing God, as well as giving a different path to understanding and appreciating *that God* has revealed himself, and *what God* has revealed.

[8] Cf. Psalm 42:7 (NSVC). The apophatic tradition is also found in such spiritual classics as *The Cloud of Unknowing* (New York: Penguin Classics, 2002) and *Pseudo-Dionysius, Complete Works* (New York: Paulist Press, 1988).

[9] Cf. Second Vatican Council, *Dei Verbum,* #2.

[10] Cf. John Paul II, *Veritatis Splendor,* #45; *Fides et Ratio,* #13, 44, 47, and 75.

[11] Pope John Paul II, *Redemptor Hominis,* #14.

[12] Cf. Second Vatican Council, *Gaudium et Spes*: "Man judges rightly that by his intellect he surpasses the material universe, for he shares in the light of the divine mind," #15.

[13] Cf. John 1:4-5 (RSVCE): "In him was life, and the life was the light of men. The light shines in the darkness, and the darkness has not overcome it." Bishop Robert Barron discussed this path of transformation, from darkness to light, in his book, *And Now I See: A Theology of Transformation* (New York: Crossroads Publishing, 1998).

[14] Cf. First Vatican Council, *Dei Filius,* Chapter Two, First Vatican Council (24 April 1870). In part, Chapter Two reads: "The same Holy Mother Church holds and teaches that God, the beginning and end of all things, can be known with certitude by the natural light of human reason from created things; 'for the invisible things of him, from the creation of the world, are clearly seen, being

understood by the things that are made' (Romans 1:20)." Cardinal Danielou took on the massive project of trying to compose the multiple and various ways that humanity can and has come to know God. The Cardinal's book, *God and the Ways of Knowing* summarized the extent and limits of reason, as well as the kindness of God who desires to reveal himself to humanity (San Francisco: Ignatius Press, 2003).

[15] Cf. First Vatican Council, *Dei Filius,* Chapter Two.

[16] Pope John Paul II made this point in reference to moral truth in *Veritatis Splendor:* "When it is a matter of the moral norms prohibiting intrinsic evil, there are no privileges or exceptions for anyone. It makes no difference whether one is the master of the world or the 'poorest of the poor' on the face of the earth. Before the demands of morality we are all absolutely equal," #96.

[17] Pope Pius XII, Encyclical *Humani Generis,* as found at vatican.va, Pius XII, Encyclicals (12 August 1950), #2.

[18] Second Vatican Council, *Dei Verbum,* #6.

[19] As contained in Romano Guardini, *Pascal for our Times* (New York: Herder, 1966), 33-44.

[20] As taught by Pope Pius XII in his encyclical *Humani Generis:* "It is well known how highly the Church regards human reason, for it falls to reason to demonstrate with certainty the existence of God, personal and one," #2.

[21] Cf. Deuteronomy 6:4-9 and 1 John 4:7-21 (RSVCE). Cf. Second Vatican Council, *Lumen Gentium,* #2; Pope Benedict XVI, *Deus Caritas Est,* #9-11. In particular, the pope wrote: "The one God in whom Israel believes, on the other hand, loves with a personal love," #9. This monumental first revelation is further developed by Etienne Gilson, *God and Philosophy* (Yale: University Press, 2002), pp. 38-73, 109-144.

[22] Plato, *Symposium,* as contained in Alexander Nehamas (Trans.), *Complete Works of Plato* (Indianapolis: Hackett Publishing Company, 1989), 201d-204c. The Judeo-Christian understanding of love is fully developed by Dietrich von Hildebrand in his masterpiece, *The Nature of Love* (South Bend: St. Augustine Press, 2009).

[23] Cf. Pope John Paul II wrote in his Apostolic Exhortation *Familiaris Consortio*: "God is love, and in Himself He lives a mystery of personal loving communion. Creating the human race in His own image and continually keeping it in being, God inscribed in the humanity of man and woman the vocation, and thus the capacity and responsibility, of love and communion. Love is therefore the fundamental and innate vocation of every human being" (#11).

[24] Cf. *Catechism of the Catholic Church*: "The mystery of the Most Holy Trinity is the central mystery of Christian faith and life. It is the mystery of God in himself. It is therefore the source of all the other mysteries of faith, the light that enlightens them. It is the most fundamental and essential teaching in the hierarchy of the truths of faith," #254.

[25] As contained and explained in Arthur Penrhyn Stanley, *The Athanasian Creed* (Charleston: BiblioBazaar, 2008); and further commented on in J.N.D. Kelly, *The Athanasian Creed* (London: Adam and Charles Black, 1964).

[26] Fr. Gerald O'Collins beautifully explained this relationship between the Persons of the Holy Trinity in his book, *The Tripersonal God* (New York: Paulist Press, 2014); Cf. Joseph Ratzinger, "Concerning the Notion of the Person in Theology," *Communio,* 17 (1990), pp. 439-454; Michael Slusser, "The Exegetical Roots of Trinitarian Theology," *Theological Studies,* 49 (1988), pp. 463-476; John Zizioulas, *Being as Communion* (New York: St. Vladimir's Seminary Press, 1985); Horst Seidl, "The Concept of Person in Thomas Aquinas," *The Thomist,* 51 (July, 1987), pp. 435-450.

[27] This notion of "gift" within the Holy Trinity is developed by Michael Downey in his book, *Altogether Gift: A Trinitarian Spirituality* (New York: Orbis Books, 2000). Fr. Raniero Cantalamessa also wrote on this point in his book, *Contemplating the Trinity* (Frederick: Word Among Us Press, 2007), especially pp. 11-24, 95-110.

[28] Cf. Pope John Paul II, *Redemptor Hominis,* #10; Pope John Paul II, *Homily,* Puebla de Los Angeles (Mexico), Palafox Major Seminary (28 January 1979).

[29] This divine pursuit is especially seen in the spiritual tradition of the Church, such as in Dom Eugene Boylan, *This Tremendous Lover* (Charlotte: TAN Books, 2013); Peter Kreeft, *The God Who Loves You* (San Francisco: Ignatius Press,

2004); and Ralph Martin, *The Fulfillment of All Desire* (Steubenville: Emmaus Road Publishing, 2006).

[30] As contained in David Scott, *Revolution of Love* (Chicago: Loyola Press, 2005), p. 16; and such a worldview is further developed in Mother Teresa, *Where There Is Love, There Is God* (London: Image Books, 2012).

[31] Pope John Paul II described the "rightful autonomy" of the human person in *Veritatis Splendor,* #40-41. In terms of an absolutized autonomy, the pope highlighted the caution of the Second Vatican Council: "For without the Creator the creature would disappear," *Gaudium et Spes,* #36.

Chapter Two

[32] As the Second Vatican Council taught, *Gaudium et Spes*: "But the Lord Himself came to free and strengthen man, renewing him inwardly and casting out that 'prince of this world' (John 12:31) who held him in the bondage of sin. For sin has diminished man, blocking his path to fulfillment," #13.

[33] John 8:12 (RSVCE): "Again Jesus spoke to them, saying, 'I am the light of the world; he who follows me will not walk in darkness, but will have the light of life.'" Cf. Galatians 4:4 (RSVCE).

[34] Cf. Genesis 1:27 (RSVCE): "God created man in his own image, in the image of God he created him; male and female he created them." Pope John Paul II discussed this original innocence and justice in his Theology of the Body, especially his Wednesday Audiences on 30 January 1980 and 13 February 1980, as contained in *Man and Woman He Created Them: A Theology of the Body* Boston: Pauline Books, 2006), pp. 190-194, pp. 198-201. Joseph Ratzinger wrote about the unique place and dignity of the human person in creation in his book, *In the Beginning: A Catholic Understanding of the Story of Creation and the Fall* (Grand Rapids: Eerdmans Publishing, 1995), pp. 41-58.

[35] Genesis 2:16-17 (RSVCE). Author Paul Kahn explored the figure of Adam and the reality of suffering in the world in his book, *Out of Eden: Adam and Eve and the Problem of Evil* (Princeton: University Press, 2009), pp. 16-53.

[36] Cf. Genesis 3:1-11 and Romans 5:19 (RSVCE). Pope John Paul II taught about original sin in his Wednesday Audience on 10 September 1986, as well as in *Veritatis Splendor*: "With this imagery, Revelation teaches that the power

to decide what is good and what is evil does not belong to man, but to God alone. The man is certainly free, inasmuch as he can understand and accept God's commands. And he possesses an extremely far-reaching freedom, since he can eat 'of every tree of the garden.'

But his freedom is not unlimited: it must halt before the 'tree of the knowledge of good and evil,' for it is called to accept the moral law given by God. In fact, human freedom finds its authentic and complete fulfilment precisely in the acceptance of that law. God, who alone is good, knows perfectly what is good for man, and by virtue of his very love proposes this good to man in the commandments," #35.

[37] Pope John Paul II described the effect of this sin on the minds and consciences of humanity in his Encyclical, *Dominum in Vivificantem* (18 May 1986), #33.

[38] Pope John Paul II addressed this topic in *Veritatis Splendor,* #35, and in his Theology of the Body, especially his Wednesday Audiences on 4 June 1980, 23 July 1980, and 30 July 1980, *Theology of the Body,* pp. 246-250, pp. 257-260, pp. 260-264. Additionally, Ratzinger wrote about the severe consequences to the person and creation by the Fall in his book, *In the Beginning,* pp. 59-79. Cf. *Catechism of the Catholic Church*: "The harmony in which [Adam and Eve] had found themselves, thanks to original justice, is now destroyed: the control of the soul's spiritual faculties over the body is shattered; the union of man and woman becomes subject to tensions, their relations henceforth marked by lust and domination. Harmony with creation is broken: visible creation has become alien and hostile to man," and #405: "[Original sin] is a deprivation of original holiness and justice, but human nature has not been totally corrupted: it is wounded in the natural powers proper to it; subject to ignorance, suffering, and the domination of death; and inclined to sin," #398.

[39] Second Vatican Council, *Gaudium et Spes,* #13.

[40] The *Catechism of the Catholic Church* uses the term "figurative language" in terms of Genesis, Chapter Three, #390.

[41] Pope John Paul II, Veritatis Splendor, #35, and the Catechism of the Catholic Church, #396-399.

[42] Pope Pius XII praised the balanced use of philosophy and human questioning in his encyclical, *Humani Generis,* #29-30, and Pope John Paul II also encouraged a moral inquiry in his encyclical, *Fides et Ratio,* #3-6.

[43] Ibid.

[44] It could be argued that the encyclical *Fides et Ratio* had as its aim the fostering and encouragement of asking questions and pursuing answers, cf. #1. The importance of knowing a philosophy of the human person, as well as right from wrong, is emphasized in Ralph McInerny, *Student's Guide to Philosophy* (Wilmington: Intercollegiate Studies Institute, 1999); and, Dietrich von Hildebrand, *The Art of Living* (Manchester: Sophia Institute Press, 1994).

[45] Cf. Pope John Paul II, Encyclical *Veritatis Splendor* (6 August 1993), #35-37, and the *Catechism of the Catholic Church* clearly taught: "The 'tree of the knowledge of good and evil' symbolically evokes the insurmountable limits that man, being a creature, must freely recognize and respect with trust. Man is dependent on his Creator and subject to the laws of creation and to the moral norms that govern the use of freedom," #396. In his Wednesday Audience on 12 November 1986, Pope John Paul II taught about the self enclosing alienation caused by sin, as found at vatican.va, John Paul II, Audiences.

[46] Cf. 1 John 5:19 and 1 Peter 5:8 (RSVCE). Pope John Paul II taught about the deformation of creation by the Fall in his Wednesday Audience on 27 August 1986, as found at vatican.va, John Paul II, Audiences. Also, Pope Pius XII confirmed the belief of the fall of human nature against challenges to it in his Encyclical *Humani Generis,* #37; and, the *Catechism of the Catholic Church* explained these teachings, #402-406.

[47] Cf. Genesis 3:5-10 (RSVCE). The *Catechism of the Catholic Church* echoed this teaching: "[Adam and Eve] became afraid of the God of whom they have conceived a distorted image – that of a God jealous of his prerogatives," #399. Ratzinger commented on this influence on the human writers of the Sacred Scriptures, *In the Beginning,* pp. 1-18. Pope John Paul II noted this tendency in his Apostolic Exhortation *Reconciliatio et Paenitentia* (2 December 1984), #10. In terms of the approach to the moral law, Pope John Paul II commented in *Veritatis Splendor,* "It follows that the authority of the Church, when she pronounces on moral questions, in no way undermines the freedom of conscience of Christians.

This is so not only because freedom of conscience is never freedom 'from' the truth but always and only freedom 'in' the truth, but also because the Magisterium does not bring to the Christian conscience truths which are extraneous to it; rather it brings to light the truths which it ought already to possess, developing them from the starting point of the primordial act of faith," #64.

[48] This perplexity is described by the Second Vatican Council, *Gaudium et Spes,* #10, and by Pope John Paul II, *Fides et Ratio,* #4, 25-28.

[49] Pope John Paul II gave an explanation of the consequences of the Fall in his Wednesday Audiences on 1 October 1986 and 8 October 1986. Cf. *Catechism of the Catholic Church*: "[Human nature] is wounded in the natural powers proper to it; subject to ignorance, suffering, and the domination of death; and inclination to sin – an inclination to evil that is called 'concupiscence,'" #405.

[50] Pope John Paul II taught on these consequences in his Theology of Body, especially his Wednesday Audiences on 24 September 1980 and 8 October 1980, *Theology of the Body,* pp. 289-292, pp. 297-301. Pope Pius XII specifically addressed the limits to natural reason because of concupiscence, *Humani Generis,* #2, and Pope John Paul II further taught about the effects of the Fall on the human mind in *Fides et Ratio,* #22.

[51] Citing St. Ambrose, Pope Benedict XVI taught about death in his encyclical, *Spe Salvi*: "Death was not part of nature; it became part of nature. God did not decree death from the beginning; he prescribed it as a remedy. Human life, because of sin ... began to experience the burden of wretchedness in unremitting labour and unbearable sorrow. There had to be a limit to its evils; death had to restore what life had forfeited," #10.

[52] Pope John Paul II, Apostolic Letter *Salvifici Doloris* (11 Feb. 1984), #7.

[53] This is one of the lessons of the Lord Jesus' answer to the apostles: "As he passed by, he saw a man blind from his birth. And his disciples asked him, 'Rabbi, who sinned, this man or his parents, that he was born blind?' Jesus answered, 'It was not that this man sinned, or his parents, but that the works of God might be made manifest in him'" (John 9:1-3).

[54] Cf. Second Vatican Council, *Gaudium et Spes,* #1-3, 10, 13; Pope John Paul II taught on this truth in *Salvifici Doloris,* summarizing his points: "Suffering is certainly part of the mystery of man," #31.

[55] Pope John Paul II taught about humanity's struggle with evil in his Wednesday Audience on 10 December 1986 and the universality of sin in human history in his Wednesday Audience on 17 September 1986, as contained in the anthology *Jesus, Son and Savior* (Boston: Pauline Books, 1996), pp. 73-77, pp. 33- 38. Author Paul Kahn also explored the reality of evil and suffering in the world in his book, *Out of Eden,* pp. 1-15.

[56] Pope John Paul II, *Fides et Ratio,* #12.

[57] Galatians 4:4-5 (RSVCE). The reality of God becoming a man was explored by many of the early Fathers, especially St. Athanasius in his book, *On the Incarnation* (New Kensington: Whitaker House, 2016). Pope John Paul II made the Incarnation and Paschal Mystery the focus of his first encyclical, *Redemptor Hominis.*

[58] John Paul II emphasized this truth in his Wednesday Audience on 27 January 1988, *Jesus, Son and Savior,* pp. 295-299. Within his teaching, the pope stressed: "Therefore, he is true God and true man, not a man merely in appearance, not a phantasm, but a true man," #8.

[59] Second Vatican Council, *Gaudium et Spes,* #22.

[60] "And the Word became flesh and dwelt among us, full of grace and truth; we have beheld his glory, glory as of the only Son from the Father," John 1:14 (RSVCE). John Paul II taught this truth in his Wednesday Audience on 26 August 1987, *Jesus, Son and Savior,* pp. 206-210. In part, he taught: "It is thus clear that, although he referred to himself especially as the Son of Man,' at the same time the whole context of what he did and taught testified that he was the Son of God in the literal sense of the term," #6.

[61] Second Vatican Council, *Dei Verbum,* #2, which reads in part: "By this revelation then, the deepest truth about God and the salvation of man shines out for our sake in Christ, who is both the mediator and the fullness of all revelation."

[62] Isaiah 6:8, John 20:21, Luke 19:10 (RSVCE). Pope John Paul II stressed the

ministry of the Lord Jesus in freeing humanity from sin in his Wednesday Audience on 27 July 1988, *Jesus, Son and Savior*, pp. 389-394.

63 "In the beginning was the Word, and the Word was with God, and the Word was God. He was in the beginning with God; all things were made through him, and without him was not anything made that was made. In him was life, and the life was the light of men. The light shines in the darkness, and the darkness has not overcome it" (John 1:1-5). Cf. Second Vatican Council, *Lumen Gentium*, #1.

64 Matthew 16:16.

65 R.V. Sellers described this history and doctrinal development in his book, *The Council of Chalcedon* (London: SPCK Publishing, 1953).

66 Council of Chalcedon, *Definition of Faith*, as contained in Norman Tanner (Trans.), *The Decrees of the Ecumenical Councils* (Georgetown: University Press, 1990), Volume I, pp. 86-87.

67 In his Wednesday Audience of 23 March 1988, Pope John Paul II emphasized the importance of the Council of Chalcedon and its Christological formula, *Jesus, Son and Savior*, pp. 331-335.

68 This point is taught by Pope John Paul II in *Catechesi* Tradendae, #9, and during his Wednesday Audience of 17 Aug. 1988, as found at vatican.va, John Paul II, Audiences. Joseph Ratzinger wrote on this truth in his essay "Jesus' Deeds and Words as the Ultimate Ethical Norm," as contained in *Principles of Christian Morality* (San Francisco: Ignatius Press, 1986), pp. 18-26.

69 Second Vatican Council, *Gaudium et Spes*, #22.

70 Dante, Paradise, Divine Comedy, Trans. Charles Eliot Norton (London: Encyclopedia Brittanica, 1952), Canto XXXIII, no. 115, p. 124.

71Cf. 1 Peter 2:9 (RSVCE). The Second Vatican Council emphasized this truth in *Dei Verbum*: "For this reason Jesus perfected revelation by fulfilling it through his whole work of making Himself present and manifesting Himself: through His words and deeds, His signs and wonders, but especially through His death and glorious resurrection from the dead and final sending of the

Spirit of truth," #4. John Paul II echoed this teaching in his encyclical *Redemptor Hominis*, #10.

[72] Cf. John: 1:9-13 (RSVCE): "The true light that enlightens every man was coming into the world. He was in the world, and the world was made through him, yet the world knew him not. He came to his own home, and his own people received him not. But to all who received him, who believed in his name, he gave power to become children of God; who were born, not of blood nor of the will of the flesh nor of the will of man, but of God." Cf. Romans 8:28-29; Hebrews 2:10- 18 and 4:15. Pope John Paul II made this point in *Salvifici Doloris:* "In his messianic activity in the midst of Israel, Christ drew increasingly closer to the world of human suffering. He went about doing good, and his actions concerned primarily those who were suffering and seeking help. He healed the sick, consoled the afflicted, fed the hungry, freed people from deafness, from blindness, from leprosy, from the devil and from various physical disabilities, three times he restored the dead to life. He was sensitive to every human suffering, whether of the body or of the soul. And at the same time he taught…," #16.

[73] Cf. Second Vatican Council, *Gaudium et Spes,* #22; Pope John Paul II, Encyclical *Redemptor Hominis,* #10, 13.

[74] Genesis 1:31 (RSVCE): "And God saw everything that he had made, and behold, it was very good." St. Thomas Aquinas especially makes the argument about privation in his treatise, *On Evil,* Trans. Richard Regan (Oxford: University Press, 2003), especially pp. 55-88. Pope Benedict XVI taught about the power of goodness and love over evil in his encyclical, *Spe Salvi,* #36-37, 47. In particular, he taught: "At the moment of judgment we experience and we absorb the overwhelming power of his love over all the evil in the world and in ourselves," #47.

[75] Hebrews 4:15 (RSVCE): "For we have not a high priest who is unable to sympathize with our weaknesses, but one who in every respect has been tempted as we are, yet without sinning."

[76] Pope John Paul II elaborated on the goodness of humanity and the effects of sin in his Apostolic Exhortation, *Reconciliatio et Paenitentia,* #14-16, 35.

[77] In his Wednesday Audience of 3 February 1988, Pope John Paul II elaborated on the Lord Jesus being without sin, *Jesus, Son and Savior,* pp. 300-304. In part,

the pope taught: "The faith of the Church is expressed as follows: He was conceived, born and died without sin," #9. The Second Vatican Council taught that the Lord is the model of our humanity, *Gaudium et Spes*, #38. Cf. Romans 15:5 (RSVCE) and Philippians 2:5 (RSVCE). Additionally, the pope in his Wednesday Audience of 10 August 1988, *Jesus, Son and Savior*, pp. 401-405, emphasized the new life that the Lord Jesus gives to us.

[78] Cf. Pope John Paul II, Encyclical *Redemptor Hominis*, #10-14.

[79] Pope John Paul II, *Homily for Seventeenth World Youth Day*, Toronto, Canada (28 July 2002).

[80] As contained in Francesca Bacardi, www.eonline.com, "Nick Confirms He's No Longer a Virgin: 'I'm an Adult,'" 20 November 2014.

[81] These teachings are especially taught by Pope John Paul II in his Theology of the Body, especially at his Wednesday Audiences on 16 January 1980, 6 February 1980, as well as on 24 September 1980, where he taught about the "depersonalizing effect" of vice, *Theology of the Body*, pp. 185-190, pp. 194-198, and pp. 289-292.

[82] Richard Norris discussed Apollinarianism in his book, *Christological Controversy* (Minneapolis: Fortress Press, 1980), pp. 79-86.

[83] Cf. Second Vatican Council, *Gaudium et Spes*, #22.

Pope John Paul II made these points in his Apostolic Letter *Salvifici Doloris*, #16, and during his Wednesday Audience on 3 February 1988, *Jesus, Son and Savior*, pp. 300-204. In part, the pope taught: "'The Word made flesh'; flesh (sarx) indicates man precisely as a corporeal being (sarkikos), who comes into being through being born of a woman (cf. Gal 4:4). In his corporeal nature Jesus of Nazareth, like every man, experienced fatigue, hunger and thirst. His body was vulnerable, subject to suffering, and sensitive to physical pain. It was precisely in this flesh (sarx) that he was subjected to dreadful tortures and was eventually crucified," #2.

[84] Various authors have illustrated the emotional and physical sufferings of the Lord. Some of the most prominent include: John Henry Newman, "The

Mental Sufferings of Our Lord in His Passion," contained in Discourses Addressed to Mixed Congregations (London: Aeterna Press, 2015); Frederick Zugibe, The Crucifixion of Jesus: A Forensic Study (London: M. Evans and Company, 2005); Pierre Barbet, A Doctor at Calvary: The Passion of Our Lord Jesus Christ as Described by a Surgeon (London: Allegro Editions, 2014).

[85] Pope John Paul II addressed these themes in his Apostolic Letter, *Salvifici Doloris,* #5, 14-16, and in his Wednesday Audience of 19 October 1988, *Jesus, Son and Savior,* pp. 438-443.

[86] Cf. Hebrews 5:8 (RSVCE): "Although he was a Son, he learned obedience through what he suffered." The Second Vatican Council, *Gaudium et Spes,* #13, 22, and Pope John Paul II taught on this subject, *Salvifici Doloris,* #20-24

[87] Cf. Pope John Paul II, *Redemptor Hominis,* #14.

[88] Philippians 2:5-11 (RSVCE): "Have this mind among yourselves, which was in Christ Jesus, who, though he was in the form of God, did not count equality with God a thing to be grasped, but emptied himself, taking the form of a servant, being born in the likeness of men. And being found in human form he humbled himself and became obedient unto death, even death on a cross. Therefore God has highly exalted him and bestowed on him the name which is above every name, that at the name of Jesus every knee should bow, in heaven and on earth and under the earth, and every tongue confess that Jesus Christ is Lord, to the glory of God the Father." Pope John Paul II taught on the Lord Jesus' sufferings and his solidarity with humanity during his Wednesday Audiences on 10 February 1988 and 17 February 1988, *Jesus, Son and Savior,* pp. 305-309, and pp. 310-314.

[89] 2 Corinthians 5:21 (RSVCE): "For our sake he made him to be sin who knew no sin, so that in him we might become the righteousness of God." At the beginning of the Lord's public ministry, St. John the Baptist greets Jesus: "Behold, the Lamb of God, who takes away the sin of the world!" (John 1:29); and, 1 Peter 2:24 (RSVCE): "He himself bore our sins in his body on the tree, that we might die to sin and live to righteousness. By his wounds you have been healed.

[90] Pope Paul VI made this observation in *Evangelii Nuntiandi,* #18, and Pope Benedict XVI elaborated on this redemption of the world when he wrote: "In Jesus' Passion, all the filth of the world touches the infinitely pure one, the soul

of Jesus Christ and, hence, the Son of God himself. While it is usually the case that anything unclean touching something clean renders it unclean, here it is the other way around: when the world, with all the injustice and cruelty that make it unclean, comes into contact with the infinitely pure one – then he, the pure one, is the stronger. Through this contact, the filth of the world is truly absorbed, wiped away, and transformed in the pain of infinite love," *Jesus of Nazareth: Holy Week* (San Francisco: Ignatius Press, 2011), p. 231.

[91] Pope John Paul II, Encyclical *Dives in Misericordia,* #7.

[92] As noted by Pope John Paul II: "The events of Good Friday and, even before that, in prayer in Gethsemane, introduce a fundamental change into the whole course of the revelation of love and mercy in the messianic mission of Christ," *Ibid.*

[93] Luke 22:39-46.

[94] Luke 15:18-19.

[95] Cf. Second Vatican Council, *Lumen Gentium,* #1-4. And Pope John Paul II explained this truth in *Dives in Misericordia,* #8, and *Redemptoris Missio,* #10.

[96] Isaiah 53:3-6; Pope Benedict XVI developed the concept of redemption in *Jesus of Nazareth,* pp. 229-240.

[97] Plato, Trans. Allan Bloom, *Republic* (New York: Basic Books, 1991), Book II, 361d-362a, pg. 39. Pope John Paul II commented on the universal appreciation of the Lord Jesus' suffering: "The suffering Christ speaks in a special way to man, and not only to the believer. The non-believer also will be able to discover in Him the eloquence of solidarity with the human lot, as also the harmonious fullness of a disinterested dedication to the cause of man, to truth and to love," *Dives in Midericordia,* #7.

[98] This understanding is developed by Pope John Paul II under the title "The Gospel of Suffering" in *Salvifici Doloris,* #25-27.

[99] Pope John Paul II elaborated on this point in *Salvifici Doloris,* under the title "Sharers in the Suffering of Christ," #19-24.

[100] Malcolm Muggeridge, *In the Valley of this Restless Mind* (New York: Harper Collins, 1978), p. 72.

[101] As contained, along with several other stories and anecdotes about the saint's life, in *Autobiography of Teresa of Avila* (Mineola: Dover Pub., 2010).

Chapter Three

[102] Cf. Luke 12: 48-51 (RSVCE): "Every one to whom much is given, of him will much be required; and of him to whom men commit much they will demand the more. I came to cast fire upon the earth; and would that it were already kindled!

I have a baptism to be baptized with; and how I am constrained until it is accomplished! Do you think that I have come to give peace on earth? No, I tell you, but rather division."

[103] This summons is exemplified in the Sermon on the Mount (Matthew 5-7) and the Sermon the Plain (Luke 6:17-49).

[104] Matthew's Gospel records one rich young man who leaves the crowds: "And behold, one came up to him, saying, 'Teacher, what good deed must I do, to have eternal life?'" Matthew 19:16 (RSVCE). The approach and the question are the initial steps to discipleship. Regrettably, this young man "went away sorrowful" Matthew 19:21 (RSVCE). Pope John Paul II used the story of this Rich Young Man for his teachings on discipleship and the moral life in *Veritatis Splendor,* #6-21.

[105] This echoes the "words and deeds" of Jesus Christ explained by the Second Vatican Council, *Dei Verbum,* #4, and developed by Pope John Paul II in *Veritatis Splendor,* #19-21, especially as the pope emphasized: "It is Jesus himself who takes the initiative and calls people to follow him," #19.

[106] Pope John Paul II, Encyclical *Redemptor Hominis,* #10.

[107] As explained by the Second Vatican Council, *Lumen Gentium*:

"In the word, in the works, and in the presence of Christ, this kingdom was clearly open to the view of men. The Word of the Lord is compared to a seed which is sown in a field; those who hear the Word with faith and become part of the little flock of Christ, have received the Kingdom itself. Then, by its own power the seed sprouts and grows until harvest time," #5.

[108] 2 Corinthians 5:17 (RSVCE). Pope John Paul II noted this conversion in *Veritatis Splendor*: "Following Christ is not an outward imitation, since it touches man at the very depths of his being. Being a follower of Christ means becoming conformed to him who became a servant even to giving himself on the Cross (cf. Phil 2:5-8). Christ dwells by faith in the heart of the believer (cf. Eph 3:17), and thus the disciple is conformed to the Lord. This is the effect of grace, of the active presence of the Holy Spirit in us." #21.

[109] Pope John Paul II, Encyclical *Veritatis Splendor,* #88.

[110] Pope John Paul II, Encyclical *Redemptoris Missio,* #46.

[111] Pope Benedict XVI, Encyclical *Deus Caritas Est,* #1.

[112] Cf. Second Vatican Council, *Lumen* Gentium: "At all times and in every race God has given welcome to whosoever fears Him and does what is right. God, however, does not make men holy and save them merely as individuals, without bond or link between one another. Rather has it pleased Him to bring men together as one people, a people which acknowledges Him in truth and serves Him in holiness," #9. Servais Pinckaers taught on this point, *Sources of Christian Ethics* (Washington, DC: Catholic University of America Press, 1995), pp.115-116, 120-125.

[113] Cf. Second Vatican Council, *Apostolicam Actuositatem,* #3-4. Pinckaers developed these points, *Sources,* pp. 117-120.

[114] This principle, based on the "two orders of knowledge," was developed by Pinckaers, *Sources,* pp. 47-94.

[115] Pinckaers explained the assimilation and transformation of the human virtues by the Christian way of life in *Sources,* 125-130; Cardinal Francis George elaborated on the call of the laity in a chapter "The Role of the Lay Faithful in Our Culture Today," as contained in his book, *The Difference God Makes* (New York: Herder and Herder, 2009), pp. 173-184.

[116] John Paul II, Apostolic Exhortation *Christifideles Laici,* #16. The *Catechism of the Catholic Church* affirms this life of the Christian believer: "He who believes in Christ becomes a son of God. This filial adoption transforms him by giving him the ability to follow the example of Christ. It makes him capable of acting rightly and doing good. In union with his Savior, the disciple attains the perfection of charity which is holiness. Having matured in grace, the moral life blossoms into eternal life in the glory of heaven," #1709.

[117] This is emphasized by Pope John Paul II in *Veritatis Splendor,* #42-45. Joseph Ratzinger wrote on this topic in his essay "Freedom, Law, and the Good," as contained in *Values in a Time of Upheaval* (San Francisco: Ignatius Press, 2006), pp. 45-52.

[118] Cf. Romans 8:5-8 (RSVCE): "For those who live according to the flesh set their minds on the things of the flesh, but those who live according to the Spirit set their minds on the things of the Spirit. To set the mind on the flesh is death, but to set the mind on the Spirit is life and peace. For the mind that is set on the flesh is hostile to God; it does not submit to God's law, indeed it cannot; and those who are in the flesh cannot please God." John Paul II taught about this slavery in *Veritatis Splendor,* #18. This gives rise to a "freedom of indifference," which Pinckaers exposed and dissected in *Sources,* pp. 327-353.

[119] St. Paul warns St. Timothy of the manipulation of truth, cf. 2 Timothy 4:1-5 (RSVCE), and the Apostle further reflects on those who abandoned moral truth and indulged in "dishonorable passions," Romans 1:24-28 (RSVCE). Pope John Paul II in his Encyclical *Dives in Misericordia* taught that one of the first actions of conscience is to call sin by its proper name, #15.

[120] Pope John Paul II, in the context of the Rich Young Man, stressed this point in *Veritatis Splendor*: "God has already given an answer to this question [about goodness]: he did so by creating man and ordering him with wisdom and love to his final end, through the law which is inscribed in his heart (cf. Rom 2:15), the 'natural law,'" #12.

[121] St. Paul teaches that the moral law has been written on the human heart: Romans 2:15 (RSVCE), and he uses the term "custodian," meaning tutor or pedagogue, in reference to the law: Galatians 3:24-25 (RSVCE). The Second Vatican Council taught these truths about the moral law in *Gaudium et Spes,*

#16, and Pope John Paul II addressed both aspects in *Veritatis Splendor,* #40, 43-45. Pinckaers developed the "pedagogical role" of the law in *Sources,* pp. 359-363.

[122] This is illustrated by Pope John Paul II regarding the Rich Young Man: "Jesus' conversation with the young man helps us to grasp the conditions for the moral growth of man, who has been called to perfection: the young man, having observed all the commandments, shows that he is incapable of taking the next step by himself alone. To do so requires mature human freedom ('If you wish to be perfect') and God's gift of grace ('Come, follow me')," #17. Pinckaers elaborated on the importance knowing right and wrong as the first step towards freedom and virtue, *Sources,* pp. 357-359.

[123] Pope John Paul II emphasized this truth in *Veritatis Splendor:* "The commandments thus represent the basic condition for love of neighbor; at the same time, they are the proof of that love. They are the first necessary step on the journey towards freedom, its starting-point," #13.

[124] Cf. *Veritatis Splendor,* #64. Pinckaers elaborates in *Sources,* pp. 330-332.

[125] Servais Pinckaers emphasized the role of the Holy Spirit and internal transformation in his book, *Morality: The Catholic View* (South Bend: St. Augustine's Press, 2003), pp. 82-95.

[126] Pickaers taught on the "freedom of excellence" and its three stages, especially the middle stage of appreciating and desiring moral goodness, *Sources,* pp. 363- 366. Cardinal Avery Dulles developed these topics in his essay "The Truth about Freedom," as contained in *Veritatis Splendor and the Renewal of Moral Theology* (Huntington: Our Sunday Visitor, 1999), pp. 129-142.

[127] Galatians 5:1.

[128] 2 Corinthians 3:17.

[129] Pope John Paul II taught: "Human freedom and God's law meet and are called to intersect, in the sense of man's free obedience to God and of God's completely gratuitous benevolence towards man," *Veritatis Splendor,* #41.

[130] Pope John Paul II noted in *Veritatis Splendor*: "Human freedom and God's law are not in opposition; on the contrary, they appeal one to the other," #17, and "God's law does not reduce, much less do away with human freedom; rather, it protects and promotes that freedom," #35.

[131] Pope John Paul II elaborated on the need for law and freedom to meet in the conscience and for virtue to flourish:

> "The relationship between man's freedom and God's law is most deeply lived out in the 'heart' of the person, in his moral conscience," *Veritatis Splendor,* #54. Pinckaers summarized these teachings, *Morality: The Catholic View,* pp. 65-81.

[132] Pinckaers discussed the development of virtue within the person in *Sources,* pp. 366-371, and gave a thorough examination of virtue in his book, *Passions and Virtues* (Washington, DC: Catholic University of America Press, 2015).

[133] Josef Pieper gave a full exposition on these theological virtues, *Faith, Hope, Love* (San Francisco: Ignatius Press, 1997).

[134] Josef Pieper provided a complete review of these primary moral virtues in *The Cardinal Virtues* (Notre Dame: University Press, 1966).

[135] Cf. 1 John 1:1-4 (RSVCE): "That which was from the beginning, which we have heard, which we have seen with our eyes, which we have looked upon and touched with our hands, concerning the word of life— the life was made manifest, and we saw it, and testify to it, and proclaim to you the eternal life which was with the Father and was made manifest to us— that which we have seen and heard we proclaim also to you, so that you may have fellowship with us; and our fellowship is with the Father and with his Son Jesus Christ. And we are writing this that our joy may be complete."

[136] Pinckaers taught that human virtue can be aspired to and exercised by all people of good will. He noted the relationship between human virtue and Christian virtue in *Sources,* pp. 168-190.

[137] Acts 8:3. Pope Benedict XVI devoted a series of Wednesday Audience talks on St. Paul. These talks have been collected under the title, *Saint Paul* (San Francisco: Ignatius Press, 2009). The Pre-Conversion life of the Apostle is addressed on pp. 13-20.

[138] Acts 9:1-2.

[139] Acts 9:4-5. Cf. Pope Benedict XVI on the Apostle's conversion, *Saint Paul,* pp. 21-25.

[140] Cf. Galatians 1:17.

[141] Cf. Galatians 1:18 and 1 Corinthians 11:23.

[142] Acts 13:2-3.

[143] Philippians 2:11. Pope Benedict XVI elaborated on the Apostle's relationship with the Lord Jesus, *Saint Paul,* pp. 43-48.

[144] Galatians 2:20.

Chapter Four

[145] The Second Vatican Council affirmed this authority of the Church in its Decree *Dignitatis Humanae,* #14, and Pope Paul VI also explained that the Church's authority extends to the natural law: "Jesus Christ, when He communicated His divine power to Peter and the other Apostles and sent them to teach all nations His commandments, constituted them as the authentic guardians and interpreters of the whole moral law, not only, that is, of the law of the Gospel but also of the natural law. For the natural law, too, declares the will of God, and its faithful observance is necessary for men's eternal salvation," *Humanae Vitae,* #4.

[146] For example, in *Dignitas Personae* the Church gave this encouragement: "The Magisterium also seeks to offer a word of support and encouragement for the perspective on culture which considers science an invaluable service to the integral good of the life and dignity of every human being. The Church therefore views scientific research with hope and desires that many Christians will dedicate themselves to the progress of biomedicine and will bear witness to their faith in this field," Congregation for the Doctrine of the Faith (20 June 2008).

[147] Cf. Second Vatican Council, *Lumen Gentium,* #8. Joseph Ratzinger taught on the role of Peter in *Called to Communion* (San Francisco: Ignatius Press, 1996),

pp. 47-52.

[148] The Second Vatican Council addressed the importance of the magisterium and adherence to the deposit of faith in unifying the Church: "Holding fast to this steadfast in the teaching of the Apostles, in the common life, in the breaking of the bread and in prayers, so that holding to, practicing and professing the heritage of the faith, it becomes on the part of the bishops and faithful a single common effort," #10. Joseph Ratzinger taught on the role and importance of the bishop: *Called to Communion,* pp. 94-104.

[149] The Second Vatican Council explained the vocation and office of the bishop, *Lumen Gentium,* #25.

[150] Cf. Second Vatican Council, *Lumen Gentium,* #32, and elaborated on by Pope John Paul II, *Christifideles Laici,* #2, 7, 20. Cardinal Avery Dulles taught on "The Nature and Function of the Magisterium" in his book, *Magisterium: Teacher and Guardian of the Faith* (Naples: Sapientia Press, 2007), pp. 1-10.

[151] The Second Vatican Council taught: "These faithful are by baptism made one own way made sharers in the priestly, prophetical, and kingly functions of Christ; and they carry out for their own part the mission of the whole Christian people in the Church and in the world," *Lumen Gentium,* #31.

[152] Cf. Romans 10:14-15, 17 (RSVCE): "But how are men to call upon him in whom they have not believed? And how are they to believe in him of whom they have never heard? And how are they to hear without a preacher? And how can men preach unless they are sent? ... So faith comes from what is heard, and what is heard comes by the preaching of Christ." Cf. *Catechism of the Catholic Church,* #875.

[153] Cf. Catechism of the Catholic Church, #890, 892.

[154] It is important to stress that when authentically understood and legitimately exercised, the magisterium is a collegial body within the community of believers: *Lumen Gentium,* #8, and Pope John Paul II, *Christifideles Laici,* which spoke of the "mystical unity" of the Church, #12.

[155] The founding of the Church by Jesus Christ was elaborated by Pope John Paul II in his Wednesday Audiences on 15 Jun. 1988 and 22 Jun. 1988.

[156] John 14:15-20 (RSVCE) and Acts of the Apostles 2:1-13 (RSVCE). Cf.

Second Vatican Council, *Apostolicam Actuositatem,* #1, 3.

[157] Cf. Catechism of the Catholic Church, #1550.

[158] Cf. Second Vatican Council, Lumen Gentium, #22-25, and Pope John Paul II continued this teaching in his Apostolic Exhortation Pastors Gregis (16 October 2003), #8.

[159] The Second Vatican Council emphasized the "words and deeds" of the Lord. These words and deeds can serve as a model for the activity of the magisterium and the entire Church, cf. *Dei Verbum,* #4.

[160] Pope John Paul II reflected on the orthopraxy of the local bishop: "The faithful ought to be able to contemplate on the face of their Bishop the grace-given qualities which in the various Beatitudes make up the self-portrait of Christ: the face of poverty, meekness and the thirst for righteousness; the merciful face of the Father and of the peaceful and peace giving man; the pure face of one who constantly looks to God alone. The faithful should also be able to see in their Bishop the face of one who relives Jesus' own compassion for the afflicted and, today as much as in the past, the face filled with strength and interior joy of one persecuted for the truth of the Gospel," *Pastores Gregis,* #18.

[161] Cf. Lumen Gentium, #46, 48; Gaudium et Spes, #42; and Apostolicam Actuositatem, #19, 24, 36.

[162] Second Vatican Council, *Lumen Gentium,* #6.

[163] Cf. Catechism of the Catholic Church, #888-892.

[164] John 15:5 (RSVCE): "I am the vine, you are the branches. He who abides in me, and I in him, he it is that bears much fruit, for apart from me you can do nothing." Pope Paul VI stressed the covenantal unity between Jesus Christ and the Church in *Evangelii Nuntiandi*: "[The Church] is the community of believers, the community of hope lived and communicated, the community of brotherly love... It is certainly fitting to recall this fact at a moment like the present one when it happens that not without sorrow we can hear people – whom we wish to believe are well-intentioned but who are certainly misguided in their attitude

– continually claiming to love Christ but without the Church, to listen to Christ but not the Church, to belong to Christ but outside the Church. The absurdity of this dichotomy is clearly evident in this phrase of the Gospel: 'Anyone who rejects you rejects me.' And how can one wish to love Christ without loving the Church, if the finest witness to Christ is that of St. Paul: 'Christ loved the Church and sacrificed himself for her?'"

#15. Joseph Ratzinger developed this understanding of "Jesus and the Church" in *Called to Communion,* pp. 21-28.

[165] 1 Corinthians 12:12-13 (RSVCE): "For just as the body is one and has many members, and all the members of the body, though many, are one body, so it is with Christ. For by one Spirit we were all baptized into one body—Jews or Greeks, slaves or free—and all were made to drink of one Spirit." The Second Vatican Council asserts: "In matters of faith and morals, the bishops speak in the name of Christ and the faithful are to accept their teaching and adhere to it with a religious assent. This religious submission of mind and will must be shown in a special way to the authentic magisterium of the Roman Pontiff," *Lumen Gentium,* #25.

[166] Cf. Romans 16:26 (RSVCE). The Second Vatican Council taught on the "obedience of faith," *Dei Verbum,* #5, and Pope John Paul II developed it further in *Fides at Ratio,* #13.

[167] Cardinal Dulles provided a thorough explanation of "The Response Due to the Magisterium," in which he explained the levels and expectations of obedience: *Magisterium,* pp. 83-100.

[168] It is important to note that the Second Vatican Council taught that the deposit of faith was entrusted to "the entire holy people," #10. The dogmatic constitution, while describing the role of the teaching office, emphasized that the deposit of faith was given to all the baptized. *Lumen Gentium,* #25, and *Apostolicam Actuositatem,* #20, did stress the necessary collaboration between the magisterium and the laity. In the most recent magisterial teaching on the Order of Bishops, the Church observed: "A lived ecclesial communion will lead the Bishop to a pastoral style which is ever more open to collaboration with all. There is a type of reciprocal interplay between what a Bishop is called to decide with personal responsibility for the good of the Church entrusted to his care and the contribution that the faithful can offer him," *Pastores Gregis,* #44.

169 The Second Vatican Council taught that the Church's truth is a good for all humanity, Decree *Dignitatis Humanae*, #14, and Pope Paul VI argued that the Church was a unique witness and expert on humanity in his Encyclical *Populorum Progessio*, #13.

170 Cf. Second Vatican Council, *Dignitatis Humanae*, #14, and Pope John Paul II stressed the mission of the Church to teach all people in his Encyclical *Redemptoris Missio*, #31.

171 Cf. Paul VI noted that the Church hopes for dialogue with all people of good will, *Ecclesiam Suam*, #93-94.

172 As proclaimed in the Pastoral Constitution *Gaudium et Spes* ("Joy and Hope"): "The joys and the hopes, the griefs and the anxieties of the men of this age, especially those who are poor or in any way afflicted, these are the joys and hopes, the griefs and anxieties of the followers of Christ," #1, and #44.

173 It could be argued that this was the mission of the Second Vatican Council. As such, *Gaudium et Spes* made these points, #3, 11, 40-45. Pope John Paul II used these points as a basis for his emphasis on "the way of man is the way of the Church," *Redemptor Hominis*, #14.

174 Cf. *Gaudium et Spes*, #4, and most explicitly in *Fides et Ratio*, #3-5.

175 Cf. First Vatican Council, *Dei Filius*, Chapter Two and Pope Pius XII, *Humani Generis*, #2; Pope John Paul II, *Fides et Ratio*, #5, 13-14. Citing Pope Pius XII, the *Catechism of the Catholic Church* provided a summary: "The precepts of the natural law are not perceived by everyone clearly and immediately. In the present situation sinful man needs grace and revelation so moral and religious truths may be known 'by everyone with facility, with firm certainty and with no admixture of error.' The natural law provides revealed law and grace with a foundation prepared by God and in accordance with the work of the Spirit," #1960.

176 Cf. *Gaudium et Spes*, #40 and Pope John Paul II, *Fides et Ratio*, #77, 92, and especially #104.

177 The Second Vatican Council noted this pastoral move by the Church,

Gaudium et Spes: "Thus, in language intelligible to each generation, [the Church] can respond to the perennial questions which men ask about this present life and the life to come, and about the relationship of the one to the other," #4. Pope John Paul repeated this call in *Fides et Ratio,* #99, 104.

[178] Joseph Ratzinger stressed this point in his essay "What is Truth? The Significance of Religious and Ethical Values in a Pluralistic Society," as contained in *Values in a Time of Upheaval* (San Francisco: Ignatius Press, 2006), pp. 53-74.

[179] Cf. Acts 1:8 (RSVCE): "But you shall receive power when the Holy Spirit has come upon you; and you shall be my witnesses in Jerusalem and in all Judea and Samaria and to the end of the earth." Cf. Second Vatican Council, *Dignitatis Humanae,* #14; Pope Paul VI, *Humanae Vitae,* #4, 27; Pope John Paul II, *Evangelium Vitae,* #80, 87; *Charter for Healthcare Workers,* #6-7.

[180] Pope Paul VI taught in *Evangelii Nuntiandi*: "[Evangelization] is a task and mission which the vast and profound changes of present-day society make all the more urgent. Evangelizing is in fact the grace and vocation proper to the Church, her deepest identity. She exists in order to evangelize, that is to say, in order to preach and teach, to be the channel of the gift of grace, to reconcile sinners with God, and to perpetuate Christ's sacrifice in the Mass, which is the memorial of His death and glorious resurrection," #14. The same pope, in *Ecclesiam Suam,* also noted: "[The limits of dialogue] stretch beyond our view into the distant horizon. It comprises the entire human race, the world. We are fully aware of the distance which separates us from the world, but we do not conceive of it as a stranger to us. All things human are our concern. We share with the whole of the human race a common nature, a common life, with all its gifts and all its problems. We are ready to play our part in this primary, universal society, to acknowledge the insistent demands of its fundamental needs, and to applaud the new and often sublime expressions of its genius. But there are moral values of the utmost importance which we have to offer it. These are of advantage to everyone. We root them firmly in the consciences of men... In all this, as we remind ourselves and others, our attitude is entirely disinterested, devoid of any temporal or political motive. Our sole purpose is to take what is good in man's life on earth and raise it to a supernatural and Christian level," #97-98, also addressing a similar topic is #106.

[181] As Pope Paul VI expressed: "The progressive development of peoples is an

object of deep interest and concern to the Church. This is particularly true in the case of those peoples who are trying to escape the ravages of hunger, poverty, endemic disease and ignorance; of those who are seeking a larger share in the benefits of civilization and a more active improvement of their human qualities; of those who are consciously striving for fuller growth," *Populorum Progressio,* #1. The delicate balance between the Church remaining true to her own confession andbeing a witness within a pluralistic society is summarized well by Pope John Paul II in *Veritatis Splendor,* #116.

[182] Second Vatican Council, *Gaudium et Spes,* #58.

[183] Cf. Philippians 4:8 (RSVCE): "Finally, brethren, whatever is true, whatever is honorable, whatever is just, whatever is pure, whatever is lovely, whatever is gracious, if there is any excellence, if there is anything worthy of praise, think about these things."

[184] Dr. Bernard Nathanson described his conversion in his book, *The Hand of God: A Journey from Death to Life* (Washington, DC: Regnery Publishing, 2013).

[185] Pope Benedict XVI expounded on this theme in *Caritas in Veritatis*: "[The Church has] a mission of truth to accomplish, in every time and circumstance, for a society that is attuned to man, to his dignity, to his vocation …Fidelity to man requires fidelity to the truth, which alone is the guarantee of freedom (cf. Jn 8:32) and of the possibility of integral human development. For this reason the Church searches for truth, proclaims it tirelessly and recognizes it wherever it is manifested. This mission of truth is something that the Church can never renounce. Her social doctrine is a particular dimension of this proclamation: it is a service to the truth which sets us free. Open to the truth, from whichever branch of knowledge it comes, the Church's social doctrine receives it, assembles into a unity the fragments in which it is often found, and mediates it within the constantly changing life-patterns of the society of peoples and nations," #9.

[186] Pope John Paul II warned about the division between faith and culture, and the importance to be diligent in one's observance of faith: *Christifideles Laici,* #59 and *Veritatis Splendor,* #116.

[187] As an example, the Congregation for the Doctrine of the Faith, *Donum Vitae,*

explained the relationship between biomedical research and the teaching of the Church, stating in part: "The Church's intervention in this field is inspired also by the Love which she owes to man, helping him to recognize and respect his rights and duties. This love draws from the fount of Christ's love: as she contemplates the mystery of the Incarnate Word, the Church also comes to understand the 'mystery of man'; by proclaiming the Gospel of salvation, she reveals to man his dignity and invites him to discover fully the truth of his own being," #1.

Chapter Five

[188] Pope Paul VI explained: "In fact the proclamation only reaches full development when it is listened to, accepted and assimilated, and when it arouses a genuine adherence in the one who has thus received it.

An adherence to the truths which the Lord in His mercy has revealed... Such an adherence, which cannot remain abstract and unincarnated, reveals itself concretely by a visible entry into a community of believers. Thus those whose life has been transformed enter a community which is itself a sign of transformation, a sign of newness of life: it is the Church, the visible sacrament of salvation," *Ecclesiam Suam,* #23.

[189] The Second Vatican Council taught: "It follows that though there are many nations there is but one people of God, which takes its citizens from every race, making them citizens of a kingdom which is of a heavenly rather than of an earthly nature. All the faithful, scattered though they be throughout the world, are in communion with each other in the Holy Spirit, and so, he who dwells in Rome knows that the people of India are his members," *Lumen Gentium,* #13.

[190] Pope John Paul II asserted at the beginning of his Encyclical *Ecclesia de Eucharistia* (17 April 2003): "The Church draws her life from the Eucharist. This truth does not simply express a daily experience of faith, but recapitulates *the heart of the mystery of the Church*," #1.

[191] The Second Vatican Council taught: "God, however, does not make men holy and save them merely as individuals, without bond or link between one another. Rather has it pleased Him to bring men together as one people, a people which acknowledges Him in truth and serves Him in holiness. He therefore chose the race of Israel as a people unto Himself. With it He set up

a covenant," #9. Joseph Ratzinger elaborated on this covenantal aspect in Chapter One of the book, *Called to Communion*. He wrote: "The institution of the most holy Eucharist on the evening before the passion cannot be regarded as some more or less isolated cultic transaction. It is the making of a covenant, and, as such, is the concrete foundation of a new people: the people comes into being through its covenant relation with God," p. 28.

[192] Pope Benedict stressed in his Wednesday Audience on 31 October 2012:

> "I cannot build my personal faith in a private dialogue with Jesus, because faith is given to me by God through a community of believers that is the Church and projects me into the multitude of believers, into a kind of communion that is not only sociological but rooted in the eternal love of God who is in himself the communion of the Father and of the Son and of the Holy Spirit, it is Trinitarian Love. Our faith is truly personal, only if it is also communal: it can be my faith only if it dwells in and moves with the 'we' of the Church, only if it is our faith, the common faith of the one Church."

[193] Pope John Paul II highlighted the "unifying power" of the Eucharist and how it fulfills the "yearning for fraternal unity deeply rooted in the human heart," *Ecclesia de Eucharistia, #23-24.*

[194] Jean-Paul Sartre as found throughout his work, *No Exit* (New York: Vintage Books, 1989).

[195] Cf. Catechism of the Catholic Church, #955.

[196] Pope John Paul II taught: "Since Christians are re-clothed in Christ Jesus and refreshed by his Spirit, they are 'holy.' They therefore have the ability to manifest this holiness and the responsibility to bear witness to it in all that they do," *Christifideles Laici, #16* (and #17).

[197] As described in Encountering the Lord in His Holy Court: A Walk Through Saint Peter's Basilica (Bethune: Signo Press, 2009), pp. 61-68.

[198] John Salza gave a thorough explanation of the Church's teachings on purgatory in his book, *The Biblical Basis for Purgatory* (Charlotte: Saint Benedict

Press, 2009).

[199] Pope Benedict XVI clarified the word "saint" in his Wednesday Audience on 31 October 2012: "Lastly, I would like, to emphasize that it is in the ecclesial community that personal faith grows and matures. It is interesting to observe how in the New Testament the word 'saints' designates Christians as a whole, and certainly not all would have qualified to be declared saints by the Church. What is meant, then, by this term? The fact that whoever had and lived the faith in Christ Risen were called to become a point of reference for all others, setting them in this way in contact with the Person and the Message of Jesus, who reveals the face of the Living God."

[200] Cf. Second Vatican Council, *Lumen Gentium:* "Nor is it by the title of example only that we cherish the memory of those in heaven, but still more in order that the union of the whole Church may be strengthened in the Spirit by the practice of fraternal charity. For just as Christian communion among wayfarers brings us closer to Christ, so our companionship with the saints joins us to Christ, from Whom as from its Fountain and Head issues every grace and the very life of the people of God," #50, as well as #40, 48, 57. Pope John Paul II also described the saints in *Ecclesia de Eucharistia,* #19 and 62.

[201] Pope John Paul II explained: "The meaning of the Church is a communion of saints. 'Communion' speaks of a double, life-giving participation: the incorporation of Christians into the life of Christ, and the communication of that life of charity to the entire body of the Faithful, in this world and in the next, union with Christ and in Christ, and union among Christians, in the Church," *Christifideles Laici,* #19.

[202] Cf. Second Vatican Council, *Sacrosanctum Concilium,* #8, 104, 111.

[203] Cf. Second Vatican Council, *Lumen Gentium,* #49 and 51. Pope John Paul II echoed the Church's cry for holiness within the Church and saints for the Church of today: "It is ever more urgent that today all Christians take up again the way of gospel renewal, welcoming in a spirit of generosity the invitation expressed by the apostle Peter 'to be holy in all conduct' (1 Pt 1:15)," *Christifideles Laici,* #16.

[204] Cf. Second Vatican Council, *Lumen Gentium,* #11; *Sacrosanctum Concilium,* #10, and Pope John Paul II, *Ecclesia de Eucharistia,* #1.

205 Cf. Second Vatican Council, *Lumen Gentium, #3.*

206 John 14:18.

207 Cf. Second Vatican Council, *Sacrosanctum Concilium, #7.*

208 Pope John Paul II noted: "The Eucharist, as Christ's saving presence in the community of the faithful and its spiritual food, is the most precious possession which the Church can have in her journey through history," *Ecclesia de Eucharistia, #9.*

209 The Second Vatican Council teaches: "Therefore all the disciples of Christ, persevering in prayer and praising God, should present themselves as a living sacrifice, holy and pleasing to God," *Lumen Gentium, #10;* Cf. *Sacrosanctum Concilium, #11, 14, 48.*

210 Pope John Paul noted: "By its union with Christ, the People of the New Covenant, far from closing in upon itself, becomes a 'sacrament' for humanity, a sign and instrument of the salvation achieved by Christ, the light of the world and the salt of the earth (cf. *Mt* 5:13-16), for the redemption of all. The Church's mission stands in continuity with the mission of Christ: 'As the Father has sent me, even so I send you' (*Jn* 20:21). From the perpetuation of the sacrifice of the Cross and her communion with the body and blood of Christ in the Eucharist, the Church draws the spiritual power needed to carry out her mission," *Ecclesia de Eucharistia, #22.*

211 Cf. Luke 24:30-35 (RSVCE): "When he was at table with them, he took the bread and blessed, and broke it, and gave it to them. And their eyes were opened and they recognized him; and he vanished out of their sight. They said to each other, 'Did not our hearts burn within us while he talked to us on the road, while he opened to us the scriptures?' And they rose that same hour and returned to Jerusalem; and they found the eleven gathered together and those who were with them, who said, 'The Lord has risen indeed, and has appeared to Simon!' Then they told what had happened on the road, and how he was known to them in the breaking of the bread." Pope John Paul stressed this point in his Apostolic Letter *Mane Nobiscum Domine* (7 October 2004), #19-24.

Cardinal Francis George elaborated on this point in his book, *The Difference God Makes,* pp. 259- 274.

[212] This basic human truth was developed by the ancient Greek philosopher, especially Aristotle in his *Politics* (Chapel Hill: University of North Carolina Press, 1997).

[213] Cf. Pope Paul VI, Encyclical *Populorum Progressio,* 17, and Pope John Paul II, Encyclical *Centesimus Annus,* as found at vatican.va, John Paul II, Encyclicals (1 May 1991), #41.

[214] These various anthropological observations and a philosophy of the human person born from them were developed by Karol Wojtyla (John Paul II), and have been collected in the book, *Person and Community* (Bern: Peter Lang Publishing, 1994).

[215] Karol Wojtyla (John Paul II) developed these principles in his book, *Love and Responsibility,* especially on pages 40-45, 139-142.

[216] For example, the Congregation for the Doctrine of the Faith reminded medical professionals of this call to community and diligent care: "As for those who work in the medical profession, they ought to neglect no means of making all their skill available to the sick and dying; but they should also remember how much more necessary it is to provide them with the comfort of boundless kindness and heartfelt charity. Such service to people is also service to Christ the Lord, who said: 'As you did it to one of the least of these my brethren, you did it to me' (Mt. 25:40)," *Declaration on Euthanasia*, Chapter IV.

[217] Benedicta Ward recounted this story and several other narratives about the Desert Fathers in her book, *Sayings of the Desert Fathers* (Collegeville: Liturgical Press, 1984).

Made in the USA
Columbia, SC
09 February 2019